CW01477045

PERFORMANCE

Stuart E. Smith

STUDY GUIDE SERIES for EASA examinations

British Library Cataloguing in Publication Data
A catalogue record for this book is pending from the British Library

First published in the United Kingdom by Cranfield Aviation Training School Limited. 2002

Further volumes in this series are:

Aircraft General Knowledge: Airframes / Systems / Powerplant / Electrics / Emergency Equipment
Air Law
Flight Planning & Monitoring
General Navigation
Human Performance
Instrumentation
Mass & Balance
Meteorology
Operational Procedures
Principles of Flight
Radio Navigation
VFR & IFR Communications

Series editor: Dr. Stuart E. Smith

CRANFIELD AVIATION TRAINING SCHOOL LTD. PART-FCL ATO N° 276
CATS INNOVATION CENTRE, LUTON, Bedfordshire LU2 8DL U.K.

www.catsaviation.com
Performance

CRANFIELD AVIATION TRAINING SCHOOL LTD. PART-FCL ATO N° 276
CATS INNOVATION CENTRE, LUTON, Bedfordshire LU2 8DL U.K.   www.catsaviation.com

Performance

ii

CHAPTER 1
Principles of Flight for Performance

1.1 The International Standard Atmosphere

Pressures and temperatures from all over the world have been averaged to form the International Standard Atmosphere.

1.1.1 Pressure in the international standard atmosphere

At sea level the pressure is 1013.25 hPa. As altitude is increased the pressure decreases on average by 27 hPa per 1000' at lower levels and 50 hPa per 1000' at higher levels. This has the effect of reducing aircraft performance.

1.1.2 Temperature in the international standard atmosphere

At sea level the temperature is 15 °C. As altitude is increased the temperature decreases on average by 1.98 °C per 1000'. This is known as a lapse rate and it is often rounded up to 2 °C per 1000' for use in calculations. This has the effect of slightly increasing aircraft performance.

1.1.3 Density in the international standard atmosphere

At sea level the density is 1225 g per m^3. As altitude is increased the density decreases. This has the effect of reducing aircraft performance.

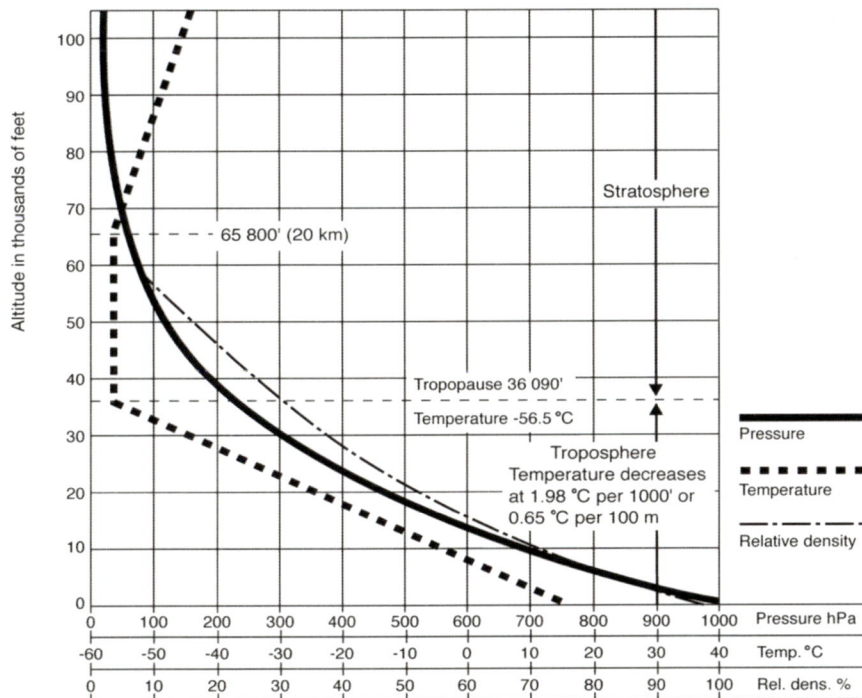

CRANFIELD AVIATION TRAINING SCHOOL LTD. PART-FCL ATO N° 276
CATS INNOVATION CENTRE, LUTON, Bedfordshire LU2 8DL U.K.   www.catsaviation.com

1-1

Performance

1.2   Airspeed relationships

Indicated airspeed is the speed that you see on the airspeed indicator. It suffers from position and instrument error. When corrected for position and instrument error it is known as Rectified or Calibrated airspeed. At low forward airspeeds air is considered to be incompressible. At higher airspeeds (above 300 KT) compressibility becomes more of an important factor and the airspeed indicator may be providing a lower than expected reading. After correction for compressibility the airspeed is known as Equivalent airspeed. Corrections for density, which changes as a function of altitude and temperature, result in True airspeed.

IAS	
	POSITION AND INSTRUMENT
RAS (CAS)	
	COMPRESSIBILITY
EAS	
	DENSITY
TAS	

$$LSS = 38.94 \sqrt{\text{Temperature K}}$$

$$MN = \frac{TAS}{LSS}$$

1.3 The effect of altitude on airspeed

1.3.1 Constant CAS

Whilst maintaining a constant calibrated airspeed in the climb, both true airspeed and Mach number increase.

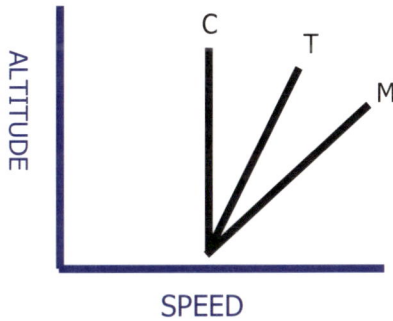

Considering the formula where IAS (or CAS) = ½ ρ V² S, as altitude increases air density decreases, this means TAS must increase to keep IAS constant. You have to travel faster to get the same pressure in the pitot tube.

Considering the formula where MN = TAS / LSS, as altitude increases air temperature decreases, this has the effect of increasing MN. Since TAS has already increased, there is a greater increase in MN.

1.3.2 Constant TAS

Whilst maintaining a constant true airspeed in the climb, calibrated airspeed decreases whilst Mach number increases.

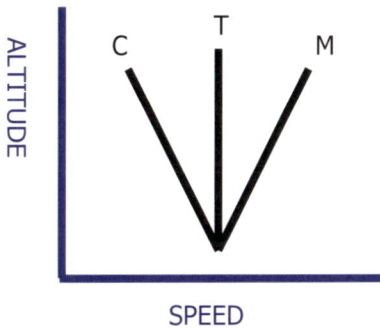

Considering the formula where IAS (or CAS) = ½ ρ V² S, as altitude increases air density decreases, however TAS has been kept constant, this means IAS (or CAS) must decrease.

Considering the formula where MN = TAS / LSS, as altitude increases air temperature decreases, with TAS held constant, a lower LSS is now divided into TAS, this has the effect of increasing MN.

1.3.3 Constant MN

Whilst maintaining a constant Mach number in the climb, both calibrated and true airspeed decrease.

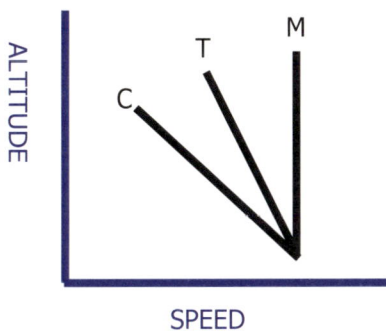

Considering the formula where MN = TAS / LSS, as altitude increases air temperature decreases, to keep MN constant TAS must decrease.

Considering the formula where IAS (or CAS) = ½ ρ V² S, as altitude increases air density decreases, since TAS has decreased, this means IAS (or CAS) must decrease even more.

1.4   The Lift Equation

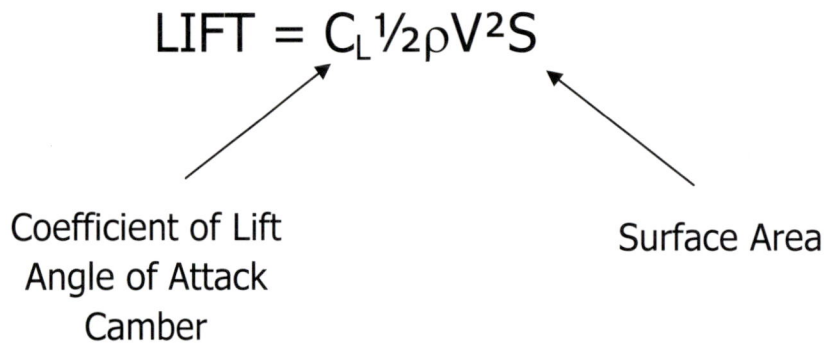

$$\text{LIFT} = C_L \tfrac{1}{2}\rho V^2 S$$

Coefficient of Lift
Angle of Attack
Camber

Surface Area

1.5   Density Altitude

Density altitude is used to determine aeroplane performance. Density altitude is pressure altitude corrected for 'non standard' temperature. Density altitude is the corresponding altitude under the given conditions on the day compared to ISA. If the temperature is higher than ISA then density altitude is higher than pressure altitude and performance is decreased. It is like operating an aeroplane at a higher altitude where the air is less dense. If the temperature is lower than ISA then density altitude is lower than pressure altitude and performance is increased. It is like operating an aeroplane at a lower altitude where the air is denser.

> Density altitude is pressure altitude corrected for 'non standard' temperature

1.6   Straight and Level Flight

Lift compensates the weight in unaccelerated straight and level flight. In level flight with constant IAS, thrust required is equal to drag. If the thrust available exceeds the thrust required for level flight the aeroplane accelerates if altitude is maintained. For this to happen the angle of attack must decrease.

To fly straight and level with reducing airspeed, angle of attack must increase. If airspeed is increasing with no change in power setting then the aircraft must be descending and pitching nose down.

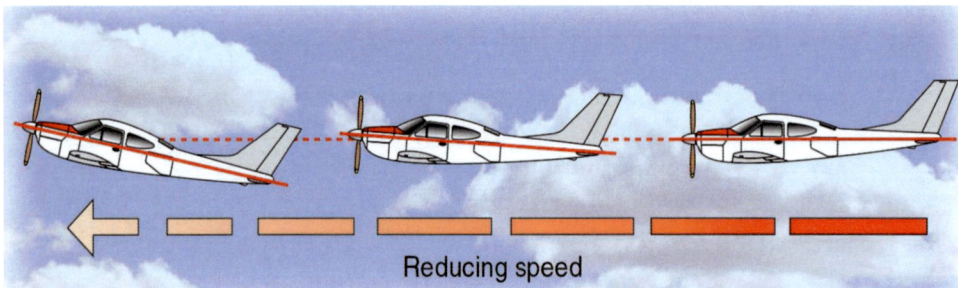

Reducing speed

To fly straight and level with reducing airspeed, angle of attack must increase

1.7   Angle of Attack

If aeroplane mass is increased more lift is required to support the weight. More lift can be achieved by increasing the coefficient of lift, increasing IAS or by increasing the surface area of the wing.

On a reciprocating engined aeroplane, to maintain a given angle of attack, configuration and altitude at higher gross mass, an increase in airspeed and power is required, and the drag will be increased.

On a reciprocating engined aeroplane, with increasing altitude at constant gross mass, angle of attack and configuration, the drag remains unchanged but the power required increases and the TAS increases by the same percentage.

1.8 The Coefficient of Lift

The coefficient of lift is a mathematical constant. It is dependent upon camber (shape of the wing) and Angle of Attack.

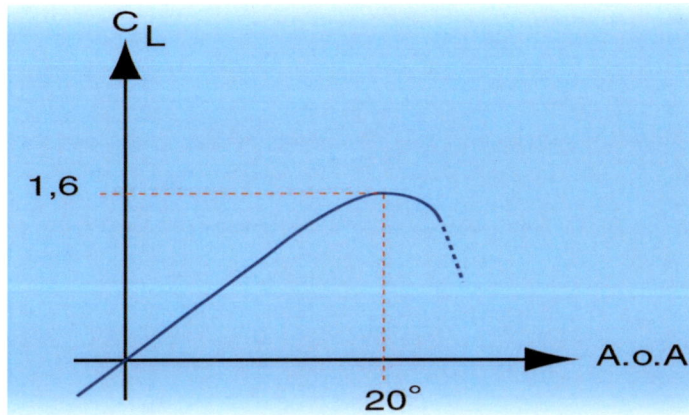

The greater the camber of a wing, the greater the coefficient of lift. The greater the Angle of Attack of a wing the greater the coefficient of lift. The coefficient of lift can be increased by flap extension which alters the shape of the wing.

> The coefficient of lift can be increased either by flap extension or by increasing the angle of attack

The lift coefficient does not vary with altitude.

1.9 The effect of airspeed on the coefficient of lift

For every angle of attack there is a particular IAS to generate the same amount of lift. If speed is increased the angle of attack can be reduced and lift will still remain the same. If speed is decreased the angle of attack can be increased and lift will still remain the same. Changes in angle of attack affect the coefficient of lift. A higher airspeed at constant mass and altitude requires a lower coefficient of lift and a lower airspeed at constant mass and altitude requires a higher coefficient of lift.

> A higher airspeed at constant mass and altitude requires a lower coefficient of lift
> A lower airspeed at constant mass and altitude requires a higher coefficient of lift

CRANFIELD AVIATION TRAINING SCHOOL LTD. PART-FCL ATO N° 276
CATS INNOVATION CENTRE, LUTON, Bedfordshire LU2 8DL U.K.   www.catsaviation.com

1-5   Performance

1.10 Induced Drag

The induced drag of an aeroplane decreases with increasing airspeed. The induced drag of an aeroplane at constant gross weight and altitude is highest at VSO (stalling speed in landing configuration).

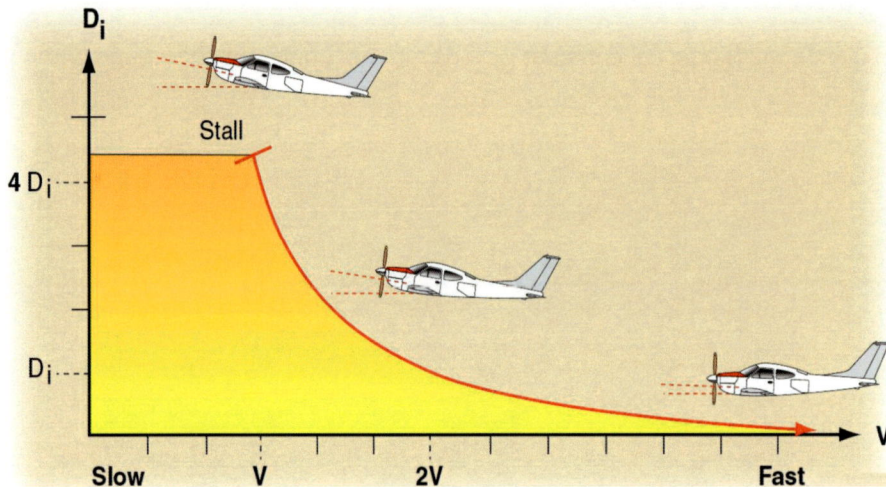

Induced drag

1.10.1 Effect of CG position on Induced drag

Moving the centre of gravity from the forward to the aft limit (gross mass, altitude and airspeed remaining unchanged) reduces the moment arm from the centre of pressure. Being less nose heavy means that less down force is required on the tailplane. Trim drag is reduced so less power is required. The angle of attack to support the weight may be decreased so induced drag is decreased.

1.11 Zero Lift Drag

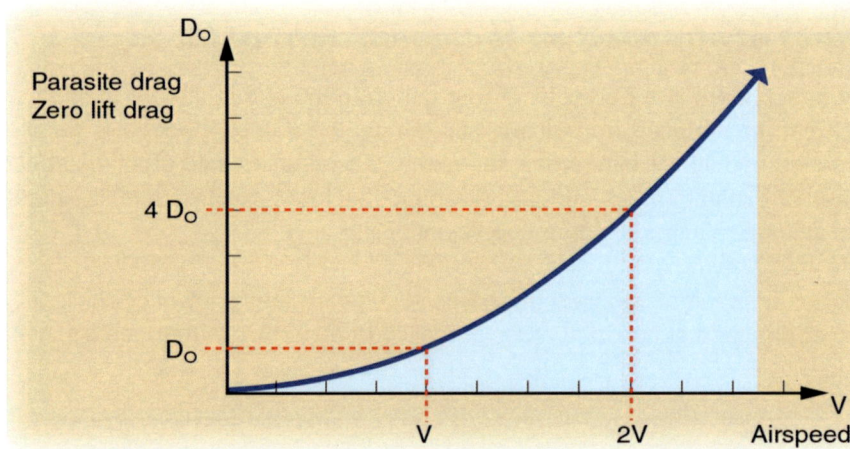

Zero Lift Drag

CRANFIELD AVIATION TRAINING SCHOOL LTD. PART-FCL ATO N° 276

CATS CATS INNOVATION CENTRE, LUTON, Bedfordshire LU2 8DL U.K.

www.catsaviation.com

1-6

Performance

1.12 Total Drag

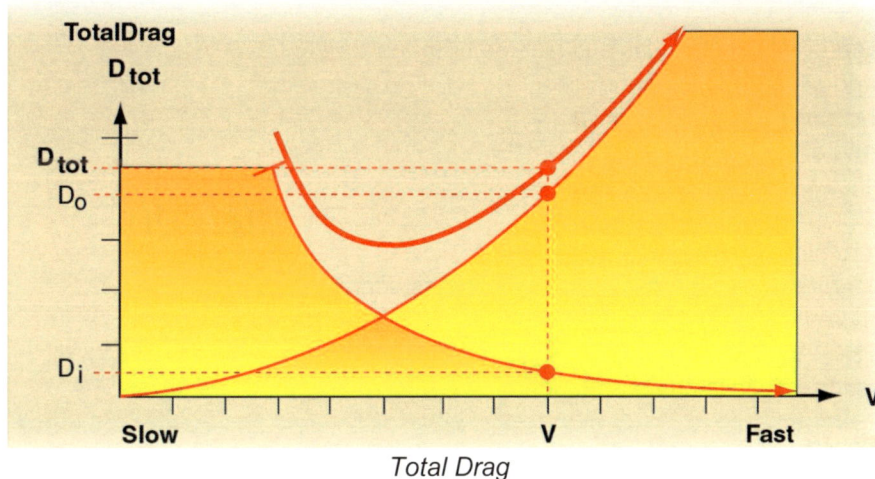

Total Drag

1.13 Velocity for Minimum Drag

The Velocity for minimum drag is at the lowest point of the total drag curve.
With regard to unaccelerated horizontal flight, minimum drag is proportional to the aircraft mass because as mass increases so does required lift to support the weight. If the aircraft mass, in a horizontal unaccelerated flight, decreases the minimum drag decreases and the IAS for minimum drag decreases.

1.14 Load Factor

The load factor in a turn in level flight depends on TAS and angle of bank. If TAS is held constant in a level turn then the load factor will only depend on bank angle.

1.15 Coefficient of Drag / Coefficient of Lift curves

The point where Drag coefficient / Lift coefficient is a minimum is the point where a tangent from the origin touches the drag curve

1.16 Power required curve

The point at which a tangent out of the origin touches the power required curve is the point where the lift to drag ratio is a maximum.

1.17 Thrust required curve

The lowest point of the thrust required curve of a jet aeroplane is the point for minimum drag.

1.18 Propeller thrust

The thrust of fixed propeller decreases slightly while the aeroplane speed builds up during take-off run

Self Assessment Test 01

1 A lower airspeed at constant mass and altitude requires:
A) more thrust and a lower coefficient of lift
B) less thrust and a lower coefficient of lift
C) more thrust and a lower coefficient of drag
D) a higher coefficient of lift

2 When flying the backside of thrust curve means:
A) a lower airspeed requires less thrust because drag is decreased
B) the thrust required is independent of the airspeed
C) a lower airspeed requires more thrust
D) a thrust reduction results in an acceleration of the aeroplane

3 How does the lift coefficient for maximum range vary with altitude? (No compressibility effects.)
A) The lift coefficient is independent of altitude
B) The lift coefficient decreases with increasing altitude
C) The lift coefficient increases with increasing altitude
D) Only at low speeds the lift coefficient decreases with increasing altitude

4 How does TAS vary in a constant Mach climb in the troposphere?
A) TAS increases
B) TAS is constant
C) TAS is not related to Mach Number
D) TAS decreases

5 Which force compensates the weight in unaccelerated straight and level flight?
A) Drag
B) Lift
C) The resultant from lift and drag
D) Thrust

6 On a reciprocating engined aeroplane, to maintain a given angle of attack, configuration and altitude at higher gross mass:
A) The airspeed will be increased but the drag does not change
B) The airspeed and the drag will be increased
C) Lift : drag ratio must be increased
D) The airspeed will be decreased and the drag increased

7 On a reciprocating engined aeroplane, with increasing altitude at constant gross mass, angle of attack and configuration:
A) the drag remains unchanged but the CAS increases
B) the drag remains unchanged but the power required increases and the TAS increases by the same percentage
C) the drag remains increases at constant TAS
D) The drag decreases and the CAS decreases because of lower air density

8 Induced drag at constant mass in unaccelerated level flight is highest at:
A) V_{MO}
B) V_{S1}
C) The lowest achievable speed at a given configuration
D) V_A

Self Assessment Test 01 Answers

1	D
2	C
3	A
4	D
5	B
6	B
7	B
8	C

CRANFIELD AVIATION TRAINING SCHOOL LTD. PART-FCL ATO N° 276
CATS INNOVATION CENTRE, LUTON, Bedfordshire LU2 8DL U.K.

www.catsaviation.com

1-9

Performance

CHAPTER 2

Take–off

032 01 00 00 PERFORMANCE OF SINGLE-ENGINE AEROPLANES NOT CERTIFIED UNDER JAR/FAR 25 (LIGHT AEROPLANES) – PERFORMANCE CLASS B

032 01 01 00 Definitions of terms and speeds used
Define the following terms:
Density altitude
Climb gradient
Unaccelerated flight
Definition of speeds in general use
Clear 50' speed (Take-off Safety Speed)
Touch down speed (Reference Landing Speed)

032 01 02 00 Take-off and Landing Performance
032 01 02 01 Effect of aeroplane mass, wind, density, altitude, runway slope, runway conditions
032 01 02 02 Use of Aeroplane flight data
Determine the following distances:
Take-off distance to 50 ft, landing distance from 50 ft , ground roll distance during landing
Climb height at given distance (of obstacle) from end of Take off Distance
Determine wind component for landing performance
Determine the take-off speeds
Determine the maximum allowed take-off weight

032 01 03 00 Climb, cruise and descent performance
Explain the effect of temperature, wind, altitude on climb performance
State rate of climb, angle of climb and minimum rate of descent and descent angle
Resolve the forces during a steady climb-, and glide
State the opposing forces during a horizontal steady flight
Explain the effect of mass and wind on the descent performance

032 01 03 01 Use of Aeroplane flight data
Determine the cruise true airspeed (TAS)
Determine the manifold air pressure (MAP)
Determine distance covered, time and fuel consumption during climb
Determine the range for certain conditions

032 01 03 02 Effect of density altitude and aeroplane mass
Explain the effect of altitude and temperature on cruise performance
Explain the effect of mass on power required, drag and airspeed
Explain the effect of altitude and temperature on the power required curve

032 01 03 03 Endurance and the effects of the different recommended power settings
Explain the effect of wind on the maximum endurance speed

032 01 03 04 Still air range with various power settings
Explain the effect of various power settings on the still air range
032 02 00 00 PERFORMANCE OF MULTI-ENGINE AEROPLANES NOT CERTIFIED UNDER JAR/FAR 25 (LIGHT TWIN) – PERFORMANCE CLASS B

032 02 01 00 Definitions of terms and speeds
Define the following terms:
Balanced/unbalanced field length
Critical engine

Speed stability, 2nd-regime or backside of power curve and normal regime
Vx speed for best angle of climb
Vy speed for best rate of climb

032 02 01 01 Any new terms used for multi-engine aeroplane performance
Explain the effect of the critical engine inoperative on the power required and the total drag
Select from a list the correct order of take-off speeds
Explain the parameter(s), which must be maintained at VMCA , in case of engine failure
Explain the effect of a clearway in take-off calculation
Explain the effect of engine failure on controllability under given conditions
State the effect for propeller- and light twin jet aeroplanes
Name the limit(s) for Vmax tire
Define V2min

032 02 02 00 Importance of performance calculations
032 02 02 01 Determination of performance under normal conditions
Explain the effect of centre of gravity on fuel consumption
Explain the effect of flap setting on the ground roll distance
For both fixed and constant speed propellers, explain the effect of airspeed on thrust during the take-off run

032 02 02 02 Consideration of effects of pressure altitude, temperature, wind, aeroplane mass, runway slope and runway conditions
Explain the effect of temperature on the brake energy limited take-off mass
Explain the effect of pressure altitude on the field length limited take-off mass
Explain the effect of runway contamination on the take-off distance
Explain the effect of mass on the speed for best angle, and best rate on the descent

032 02 03 00 Elements of performance
Discuss the aeroplane's CL / CD curve for specified configurations
Explain the certified engine thrust ratings
Explain the effect of temperature and altitude on the fuel flow for jet engine aeroplanes in given conditions
Explain the effect of bank angle at constant TAS on the load factor
Explain the effect of wind on the maximum range speed and speed for maximum climb angle
Explain the effect of mass on descent performance
Explain the effect of airspeed on the thrust of a jet engine aeroplane at constant RPM
Explain the effect of speed and angle of attack on the induced drag
Interpret the 'thrust required' and' thrust available' curves
Interpret the 'power required' and 'power available' curves
State and explain specific range (SR) and aeroplane's specific fuel consumption (SFC)

032 02 03 01 Take-off and landing distances
Explain the effect of thrust reverser on take-off mass calculation
State the percentage of accountability for head, and tailwind during take-off calculations
Determine landing distance required (dry and wet) for destination and alternate airports valid for jet- and propeller aeroplanes

032 02 03 02 Rate of climb and descent
Explain the effect of selected power settings, speeds, mass and flaps on the rate of climb versus airspeed curve
Explain the effect of mass, altitude and flaps on the idle descent

032 02 03 03 Cruise altitude and altitude ceiling
Define service, and absolute ceiling and optimum altitude
Explain effect of altitude, mass, configuration on total drag under given conditions
Interpret the Buffet onset Boundary Chart (BOB-chart)
Describe manoeuvring capability, low, and high speed limits
Indicate effects of mass and bank angle in the BOB-chart
Identify buffet onset gust factor

032 02 03 04 Payload/range trade-offs
Interpret the payload-range diagram
Describe cruise technique, and meteorological conditions

032 02 03 05 Speed/Economy trade-off
Explain the correlation between maximum endurance and fuel consumption

032 02 04 00 Use of performance graphs and tabulated data
Explain the effect of brake release before take off power is set on the accelerate, and stop distance

032 03 00 00 PERFORMANCE OF AEROPLANES CERTIFIED UNDER FAR/JAR 25 – PERFORMANCE CLASS A JAR 25.105

032 03 01 00 Take – off
Explain the essential forces affecting the aeroplane during take-off until lift off
State the effects of angle of attack, thrust-to-weight ratio and flap setting on acceleration distance

032 03 01 01 Definitions of terms and speed used
Define the following speeds: IEM FCL 1.475(b)
VMC : minimum control speed JAR 25.149 (a thru d)
VMCG : ground minimum control speed JAR 25.149 (e)
VMCA : air minimum control speed JAR 25.149
VEF : engine failure speed JAR 25.107(a) (1)
V1 : critical engine failure speed (decision) JAR 25.107(a) (2)
VR : rotating speed JAR 25.107 (e)
V2 : take-off safety speed for piston engine aircraft, or take-off climb speed or speed at 35 ft for jet Aircraft JAR 25.107(b) (c)
VMU : minimum unstick speed JAR 25.107 (d) and (e)
VLOF : lift off speed JAR 25.107 (f)
VMBE : max brake energy speed
V Max Tyre : max tyre speed
VS : stalling speed or minimum steady flight speed at which a/c is controllable
Distinguish VS0 & VS1
Define the following distances: JAR 25.113
TORA & TORR : 'Take off run available' & 'Take off run required' with all engines operating and one engine inoperative
TODA & TODR: 'Take off distance available' & 'Take off distance required' with all engines operating and one engine inoperative JAR 25.113
ASDA & ASDR: 'Accelerate stop distance available' & 'Accelerate stop distance required'
Clearway and stopway JAR 25.109
Define balanced field length

032 03 01 02 Runway variables
Explain the effects of the following runway variables on take off performance dimensions, slope, surface condition (damp, wet or contaminated), PCN , field elevation, influence of contamination on friction coefficient

032 03 01 03 Aeroplane variables
Explain the effects of the following aeroplane variables on take off performance
mass, configuration, variable power settings, reduced thrust, serviceability of high lift devices, application of reverse thrust, brakes and use of anti-skid devices

032 03 01 04 Meteorological variables
Explain the effects of the following meteorological variables on take off performance wind components (along and across runway), precipitation, temperature and pressure altitude - wing icing – windshear

032 03 01 05 Take off speeds
Explain the significance and applicability of the take off and initial climb 'V' speeds for specified conditions and configuration for all engines operating and one engine inoperative
State V1 , VR , V2 , V2 + increment , landing gear and flap/slat retraction speeds

State upper and lower limits of the take off speeds V1 , VR and V2
State the reaction time between engine failure and recognition
Elaborate on factors which affect V2
State mass, temperature, elevation and flap setting
Explain the effect of pressure altitude on VMCA
Explain the effect of increasing altitude on the stall speed (IAS)

032 03 01 06 Take off distance
Explain the significance and applicability of the take off distances for specified conditions and configuration for all engines operating and one engine inoperative
the influence of aeroplane-, runway- and meteorological variables
the effect of early/late rotation of the aeroplane
Explain the effect of using clearway on the take-off distance required
Explain the effect of miscalculation of V1 on the take-off distance required
Explain the effect of using a higher or lower V1 than the balanced V1 on the take-off distance
Explain effect of higher flap setting on the average drag during the acceleration distance

032 03 02 00 Accelerate-stop distance
Explain the significance and applicability of the accelerate-stop distance for specified conditions and configuration for all engines operating and one engine inoperative
Explain the influence of aeroplane, runway and meteorological variables
Explain the effect of using a stopway on the accelerate-stop distance required
Explain the effect of miscalculation of V1 on the accelerate-stop distance required
Explain the effect of using a higher or lower V1 than the balanced V1 on the accelerate-stop distance and action(s) to be taken in case of engine failure below V1

032 03 02 01 Concept of balanced field length
Explain the significance and applicability of a balanced/unbalanced field length
Explain the effect of a stopway on the allowed take off mass and appropriate V1
Explain the effect of a clearway on the allowed take off mass and appropriate V1
State relation of take off distance, accelerate stop distance and V1
Elaborate on the runway length limited take-off mass (RLTOM)

032 03 02 02 Use of flight manual charts
Using the aeroplane performance data sheets, compute the accelerate stop distances, decision time and deceleration procedure assumptions
Explain time-to-decide allowance, use of brakes, use of reverse thrust, brake energy absorption limits, delayed temperature rise and tyre limitations - fuse plug limit
Explain the typical form of the wind guide lines in the performance charts
Explain the effect of anti-skid u/s during take-off
Explain the effects of runway, aeroplane and meteorological variables on the tyre speed limited take off

032 03 03 00 Initial climb
Define gross,- and net take-off flight path with one engine inoperative
State the effects of runway-, aeroplane,- and meteorological variables on determination of climb limited take-off mass (CLTOM) and obstacle limited take-off mass (OLTOM) JAR 25.111-115-117-121-123
Explain the use of 35 ft vertical distance over obstacles and equivalent reduction in acceleration at the point at which the aeroplane is accelerated in level flight

032 03 03 01 Climb segments
Define the segments along the gross take-off flight path
State distinct changes in the configuration, power or thrust, and speed
State distinct differences in climb gradient requirements for various types of aeroplanes during
State maximum bank angle when flying at V2
Determine the climb limited take-off mass (CLTOM) given relevant data performance

032 03 03 02 All engines operating
Calculate by means of a rule of thumb the rate of climb of the aeroplane

Calculate the climb gradient for a given Lift/Drag ratio, thrust, mass and gravitational acceleration (G)

Describe the noise abatement procedures A and B during take-off according to PANS-OPS

032 03 03 03 Engine inoperative operation

Explain the effects of aeroplane and meteorological variables on the initial climb

Consider influence of airspeed selection, acceleration and turns on the climb gradients, best rate of climb speed and best angle of climb speed

Computation of maximum take-off mass at a given minimum gross gradient (2nd segment) sin of angle of climb, thrust per engine, G and drag

032 03 03 04 Obstacle clearance requirements

Distinguish difference between the Obstacle Limited Take off mass (OLTOM) and Climb Limited Take off mass (CLTOM)

State the operational regulations for obstacle clearance of the net take-off flight path in the departure sector

032 03 04 00 Climb

Explain the effect of climbing with constant Mach Number on the lift coefficient

Explain the effect of climbing with constant IAS on the drag

Explain the effect of mass on the Rate of Climb (ROC) speed

Computation of the maximum climb speed by using performance data

Explain the effect of meteorological variables on the ground distance during climb

032 03 04 01 Use of flight manual performance charts

Distinguish the difference between the flat rated and non flat rated part in performance charts

Elaborate on the cross over altitude, during a certain climb speed schedule (IAS-Mach Number)

032 03 04 02 Significant airspeeds for climb

Give, from a list, the correct sequence of speeds for jet transport aeroplanes

State the effect of mass on VX and VY

State the effect on TAS when climbing in and above the troposphere at constant Mach Number

State the effect of meteorological variables on the climb speeds

State the effect on the operational speed limit when climbing at constant IAS

State the effect of flaps on VX and VY

State the effect of acceleration on VX and VY at a given constant power setting

032 03 05 00 Cruise

Explain the relationship between mass and minimum drag during a steady horizontal flight

Explain and state the factors which affect the optimum long range cruise altitude

Explain the relationship between airspeed and induced drag

032 03 05 01 Use of cruise charts

Explain in detail the Buffet Onset Boundary Chart (BOB-chart)

State influence of bank angle, mass and 1.3 g buffet onset factor on the step climb

Explain the purpose of step climbs used on long distance flights

Explain and state factors which affect the choice of optimum altitude

Explain the factors which might affect or limit the maximum operating altitude

032 03 05 02 Cruise control

Explain differences in flying Vlong range and Vmax range with regard to fuel flow and speed stability

Discuss 'thrust/power available and required' curves in horizontal flight

Explain reasons for flying above or below optimum altitude

Computation of fuel consumption in relation to different aeroplane masses

Explain the difference between Specific Fuel Consumption (SFC) and Specific Range (SR)

Computation of fuel mileage

Explain the factors which affect the thrust/power available and thrust/power required curves in horizontal flight

032 03 05 03 En-route One Engine Inoperative JAR 25.123

Explain in detail the drift-down procedure JAR-OPS 1.580

Identify factors which affect the en-route net flight path

State minimum obstacle clearance height prescribed in JAR-OPS 1.580
Explain influence of deceleration on the drift-down profiles
Explain the effect of one engine inoperative at high altitudes on the SFC and SR and drift-down speed

032 03 05 04 Obstacle clearance en-route
Explain items mentioned in 032 03 05 04 JAR 25.123

032 03 05 05 En-route – Airplanes with three or more Engines, two engines inoperative
Analyse critical situation
State factors which affect the requirements and limitations:
Limited systems operations
Raised landing weather minima
Cross wind limits
Reduced range
Highly reduced aeroplane performance

032 03 06 00 Descent and landing JAR 25.119, 121 and 125
Explain the effect of changing lift coefficient during glide at constant Mach Number
Describe effect of pitch changes on the glide distance
Explain the influence of mass, configuration, altitude on rate of descent, glide angle and lift/drag ratio
Resolve the forces during a steady idle-descent (glide) flight
Explain the effect of a descent at constant Mach Number on the margin to low speed and Mach buffet
State the requirements for establishing VREF and VT
State the requirements for the approach and landing climb limits
State the requirements for the maximum landing distance (dry and wet) applicable for turbo propeller and turbojet aeroplanes at both destination and alternate
Explain the relationship between mass, pitch angle, airspeed and lift/drag ratio during a glide

032 03 06 01 Use of descent charts
Explain the effects on Mach Number and airspeed (IAS) during a descent schedule
Explain the effect of mass on the vertical speed and forward speed at given conditions
Identify the difference between VMO - VNE – MMO

032 03 06 02 Maximum permitted landing mass
Explain factors as mentioned in the subject Mass & Balance
Demonstrate knowledge of brake energy limited landing weight - overweight landing – flap placard speed - limiting bank angle - landing distance required

032 03 06 03 Approach and landing data calculations
Explain the effect of hydroplaning on landing distance required a. JAR-OPS
State three types of hydroplaning b. JAR 25
Suitability of selected landing runway landing distance available c. Appropriate aeroplane
Computation of maximum landing mass for the given runway conditions Performance data sheets
State the requirements for determination of maximum landing mass
Determine, using aeroplane performance data sheets, the maximum landing mass for specified runway and environmental conditions
Computation of the minimum runway length for the given aeroplane mass condition
State the requirements for determination of minimum runway length for landing
Determine, using aeroplane performance data sheets, the minimum runway length for a specified landing mass, runway and environmental conditions
Other factors: runway slope, surface conditions, wind, temperature, pressure altitude, PCN
Explain the effect of runway slope, surface conditions and wind and how each factor modifies the maximum landing mass for given runway distance and landing distance required for given landing mass
Explain the effect of temperature and pressure altitude and how they modify the maximum landing mass for given runway distance and landing distance required for given landing mass
Explain the effect of temperature and pressure altitude on approach and landing climb performance
Explain the limitations that may be imposed when ACN > PCN
Computation of expected landing mass

CRANFIELD AVIATION TRAINING SCHOOL LTD. PART-FCL ATO N° 276
CATS INNOVATION CENTRE, LUTON, Bedfordshire LU2 8DL U.K.   www.catsaviation.com

2-6   Performance

Using the aeroplane performance and planning data sheets calculate the expected landing mass for specified basic weight, load and fuel requirements

Computation of approach and landing speeds

Explain the factors affecting the determination of approach and landing speeds

Using aeroplane performance data sheets determine approach and landing speeds for specified landing masses, configuration and conditions

Computations for alternate aerodromes

Explain the requirements for alternate aerodromes

Using aeroplane performance data sheets determine approach and landing speeds for specified landing masses, configuration and conditions

Definitions of terms and speeds used

VT - threshold speed JAR

Explain the factors used in determination of VT

Discontinued approach climb

Explain the requirements and aeroplane configuration for the discontinued approach climb

Landing climb

Explain the requirements and aeroplane configuration for the landing climb

Landing distance, dry, wet and contaminated runways

Explain the factors to be considered in determining the landing distance required for dry, wet and contaminated runways

Landing distance required

State the destination and alternate aerodrome landing distance requirements for turbojet and turbo-prop aeroplane

In each case state the requirements for turbojet and turbo-prop aeroplanes

State the limitations on dispatching an aeroplane if the landing requirements at the destination aerodrome are not met

Landing climb performance

State the minimum performance requirement for landing climb

Landing configuration

State the requirements for landing with all engine operating and one engine inoperative

Approach configuration

State the requirements for the approach configuration with all engines operating and one engine inoperative

032 03 07 00 Practical application of an airplane performance manual
032 03 07 01 Use of typical turbojet or turboprop aeroplane performance manual

Take-off, en-route and landing mass calculation a. JAR-OPS

Determine from the aeroplane performance data sheets the maximum weights which satisfy all the regulations for take-off, en-route and landing given the appropriate conditions

b. JAR 25

c. Appropriate aeroplane

Take-off data computations Performance data sheets

Effects of runway variables, aeroplane variables and meteorological variables

Explain the effect on aeroplane performance and operating weights of the following:

Runway: dimensions, slope, surface condition, PCN

Aeroplane: configuration, variable power settings, serviceability of high lift devices, reverse thrust, brakes and anti-skid devices

Meteorological Conditions: wind components (along and across runway), precipitation, temperature and pressure

Computation of the relevant 'V' speeds for take-off and initial climb

Explain the significance and applicability of the take-off and initial climb 'V' speeds

Using the aeroplane performance data sheets determine the relevant speeds for specified conditions and configuration for all engines operating and one engine inoperative

Computation of runway distance factors

Determine the effective length of the runway for specified configuration, runway and meteorological conditions for all engines operating and one engine inoperative, using the aeroplane performance data sheets

Determination of rate and gradient of initial climb

Using the aeroplane performance data sheets determine the rate and gradient of climb with all engines operating and one engine inoperative for specified configuration and meteorological conditions

Determination of obstacle clearance

Using the aeroplane performance data sheets determine the maximum mass at which obstacles can be cleared for specified conditions to comply with the regulations for all engines operating and one engine inoperative

Appropriate engine out calculations

Using the aeroplane performance data sheets determine the aeroplane performance with all engines operating and one engine inoperative, for specified conditions
Climb computations
In each of the following, accurately extract the information from the aeroplane performance data sheets for the all engines operating and one engine inoperative cases
Climb rates and gradients
Time to climb
Fuel used

032 03 07 02 Cruise computations
Power settings and speeds for maximum range, maximum endurance, high speed and normal cruise
a. JAR-OPS
b. JAR 25
Explain the effect on aeroplane range, endurance and fuel consumption of power setting/speed options
State the factors involved in the selection of cruise technique accounting for cost indexing, passenger requirements against company requirements
c. Appropriate aeroplane
Extract the power settings and speeds from the aeroplane performance data sheets
Fuel consumption
Extract the fuel consumption figures from the aeroplane performance data sheets
Engine out operations, pressurisation failure, effect of lower altitude on range and endurance
Explain the effect on aeroplane operations of engine failure, pressurisation failure, effect of lower altitude on range and endurance
Extended Twin Operations (ETOPS)
State the additional factors to be considered for ETOPS
Additional consideration concerning fuel consumption
Effects of altitude and aeroplane mass
Explain the effect on fuel consumption of altitude and aeroplane mass
Fuel for holding, approach and cruise to alternate
Determine the fuel requirements for holding, approach and transit to an alternate from the aeroplane performance data sheets in normal conditions and the following abnormal conditions
After engine failure, After decompression

2.1 Objective

The objective of performance planning is to provide a margin of safety between the performance capabilities of the aeroplane and regulatory requirements affecting which it during each stage of flight.

Measured performance is the average performance of an aeroplane or group of aeroplanes undergoing test by an acceptable method under specified conditions

Gross performance is the average performance that a fleet of aeroplanes should achieve if satisfactorily maintained and flown, by pilots of average ability, in accordance with the techniques described in the Aircraft Flight Manual

Net performance is gross performance diminished by safety factors to allow for contingencies that cannot be accounted for operationally, such as variations in pilot technique

The aeroplane's performance capabilities are determined by the manufacturer and reported in the Performance Section of the Aircraft Flight Manual. The required safety margin is dictated by JAA documents JAR-OPS 1 Subparts F to I and, for large turbine-powered aeroplanes, JAR 25.

CRANFIELD AVIATION TRAINING SCHOOL LTD. PART-FCL ATO N° 276
CATS CATS INNOVATION CENTRE, LUTON, Bedfordshire LU2 8DL U.K.   www.catsaviation.com

2-8   Performance

2.2 JAR Performance Classification

There are 3 main aircraft performance classes described in JAR-OPS 1.470.

Performance Class A	multi-engine turboprop aeroplanes with a maximum approved passenger seating configuration of more than 9 or a maximum take off mass exceeding 5700 kg and all multi-engine turbojet aeroplanes	B737-400
Performance Class B	propeller-driven aeroplanes with a maximum approved passenger seating configuration of 9 or less and a maximum take off mass of 5700 kg or less	Beech Bonanza, Seneca III
Performance Class C	aeroplanes powered by reciprocating engines with a maximum approved passenger seating configuration of more than 9 or a maximum take off mass exceeding 5700 kg	

Aeroplanes in Performance Class A, in the event of a critical power unit failure at any point during take off, must be able to either stop or continue to a height of 1500' above an aerodrome, while clearing obstacles by given margins. They may also operate from contaminated runways and with certain configuration deviations. IEM OPS 1.535 states that manufacturers of multi-engined aeroplanes in Performance Class B need not provide data to account for an engine failure below 300'. Single engine aeroplanes in Performance Class B are restricted to routes that allow a safe forced landing to be executed and are prohibited from operating at night or in IMC, except under SVFR.

2.3 The sequence of speeds during take off

For any aeroplane with a fixed lifting surface, the lift developed depends on the lift coefficient C_L and on the dynamic pressure $\frac{1}{2} \rho v^2$.

$$\text{Lift} = c_L \; \frac{1}{2} \rho \; v^2 \; S$$
ρ is the air density, V the true airspeed (TAS) and S the surface area of the wings

2.4 V_s

Stalling speed is such an important speed for an aircraft that many other speeds are based upon it. The calibrated stall speed, V_S, is not less than 94% of the minimum calibrated airspeed (CAS) at which an aeroplane can develop lift equal to its own weight. V_{S0} is the calibrated stall speed with flaps set for landing. V_{S1} is the calibrated stall speed with the aeroplane in the configuration appropriate to the case under consideration.

The speed VS is defined as stalling speed or minimum steady flight speed at which the aeroplane is controllable

The speed VSO is defined as the stalling speed or the minimum steady flight speed at which the aeroplane is controllable in landing configuration

The speed VS1 is defined as the calibrated stall speed with the aeroplane in the configuration appropriate to the case under consideration

For aeroplanes in Performance Class A, reference stall speeds V_{SR} and V_{SR0}, clean and in the landing configuration respectively, are defined by JAR 25 to account for the activation of a device that abruptly pushes the nose down at a selected angle of attack (a stick pusher). Since the stick pusher activates before the effects of the stall would normally become significant, V_{SR} is approximately 6% faster than V_S. To prevent existing performance graphs using original safety factors becoming obsolete, other speeds based on the stall speed, are also reduced by the same margin, that is, multiplied by 0.94.

> V_{SR} is defined as the reference stall speed and may not be less than the 1g stall speed

Whereas previously, then, V_{MC} for aeroplanes in Performance Class A was required by JAR 25.149 to be not greater than 1.2 V_S, the introduction of V_{SR} requires that it be now not greater than 0.94 times 1.2 V_{SR}.

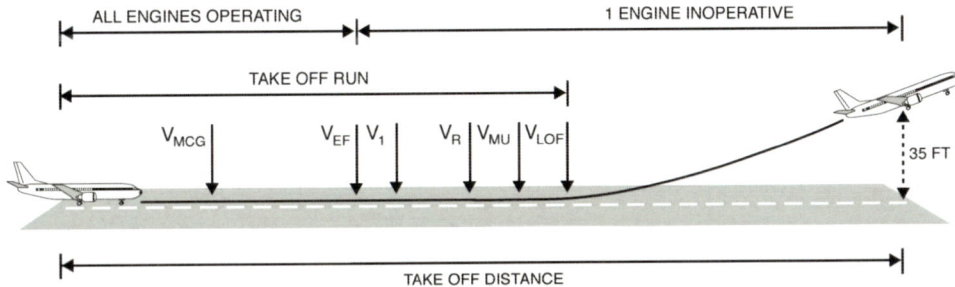

Figure 1.1 The sequence of speeds V_{MCG}, V_{EF}, V_1, V_R, V_{MU} and V_{LOF} during take off

> $V_{MCG} \leq V_{EF} < V_1$

> $V_S < V_{MCA} < V_{2min}$

2.5 Critical Engine

If an engine fails during take off in a multi-engine aeroplane a significant yawing moment is experienced due to asymmetric thrust. Above a certain speed, correction is possible using aerodynamic controls alone. On the ground only the rudder is available, however once airborne the pilot may also apply bank towards the live engine using ailerons. With a critical engine inoperative the power required increases because of the greater drag caused by the wind-milling engine and the compensation for the yaw effect. The engine that causes the largest yawing moment upon failure is called the critical engine. When the aeroplane is airborne, the moment required to compensate asymmetric thrust will depend not only on the aerodynamic force generated by the rudder, a function of the airspeed, but also on the moment arm, that is the distance between the aeroplane's centre of gravity and the rudder where the aerodynamic force is applied.

> The critical speed is higher with an aft centre of gravity because the moment arm is shorter

On the ground, the moment arm is given by the distance from the main wheels to the point of application of the aerodynamic force. The critical speed on ground is therefore not affected by the location of the centre of gravity.

2.6 V_{MCG}

V_{MCG} is the lowest CAS on the ground at which, at maximum take off power, when the critical engine suddenly becomes inoperative, it is possible to maintain control using primary aerodynamic controls alone in order to continue the take off. JAR 25.149(e) states that, following engine failure, the aircraft must not deviate more than 30' laterally from the runway centreline.

> Minimum control speed on ground, V_{MCG}, is based on directional control being maintained by primary aerodynamic control only

CRANFIELD AVIATION TRAINING SCHOOL LTD. PART-FCL ATO N° 276

CATS CATS INNOVATION CENTRE, LUTON, Bedfordshire LU2 8DL U.K.

www.catsaviation.com

2-10

Performance

2.7 V_{MC}

V_{MC} is the lowest CAS at which, when the critical engine suddenly becomes inoperative, it is possible to maintain straight flight with an angle of bank not exceeding 5° and without a change of heading of more than 20°.

2.8 V_{MCA}

V_{MCA} is the minimum control speed in the take off climb. If a multi engine aeroplane is flying at the minimum control speed V_{MCA} straight flight must be maintainable after engine failure.

JAR 25.149(b), (c) and (d) and ICAO Annex 6 state that

$$V_{MCG} \; < \; V_{MC} \; \leq \; \begin{array}{l} 1.2\,V_S \\ 1.13\,V_{SR} \end{array}$$

V_{MCG} and V_{MC} are a function only of air density

2.9 V_{EF}

V_{EF} is the CAS at which the critical engine of aeroplanes in Performance Class A is assumed to fail.

JAR 25.107(a) states that:

$$V_{MCG} \; \leq \; V_{EF} \; < \; V_1$$

2.10 V_1

The speed V1 is defined as take-off decision speed

The decision speed V_1 is a speed from which an aeroplane in Performance Class A, following failure of the critical engine, shall be able either to stop safely or to safely become airborne. The take-off decision speed V_1 is a chosen limit. If an engine failure is recognized before reaching V_1 the take-off must be aborted.

The take-off decision speed V_1 is the airspeed on the ground at which the pilot is assumed to have made a decision to continue or discontinue the take-off

In the event of engine failure below V_1, the first action to be taken by the pilot in order to decelerate the aeroplane is to reduce the engine thrust. There is a two-second delay built into V_1 to allow for the recognition of and reaction to the engine failure by the pilot. If the engine failure is recognized at a speed lower than V_1 the take off should normally be rejected. If the engine failure is recognized at a speed higher than V_1 the take off should normally be continued. There may be a speed range for V_1 for a given runway and aeroplane mass. It is not realistic to try to stop the aeroplane once rotation has been initiated. Conversely, should the critical engine fail at a speed lower than V_{MCG}, the pilot must reject the take off because the aeroplane is then not controllable with aerodynamic controls alone.

$$\left(V_{EF} + \text{speed increase after engine failure}\right) \; \leq \; V_1 \; \leq \; \begin{array}{l} V_R \\ V_{MBE} \end{array}$$

where V_{MBE} is the maximum speed on the ground from which the aircraft can be safely stopped within the energy-absorbing capability of the brakes

2.11 V_R

V_R is the speed at which rotation should be initiated. At rotation speed V_R the nosewheel lifts off. A usual mean rate of rotation is 3° per second for large transport aeroplanes.

For aeroplanes in Performance Class A
$$V_R \geq \begin{array}{l} V_1 \\ 1.05\,V_{MC} \end{array}$$

For single engine aeroplanes in Performance Class B
$$V_R \geq V_{S1}$$

For twin engine aeroplanes in Performance Class B
$$V_R \geq \begin{array}{l} 1.1\,V_{S1} \\ 1.05\,V_{MC} \end{array}$$

V_{MU} is the lowest possible unstick speed, V_{US}, at which it is possible to leave the ground and climb safely to screen height with all power units operating.

2.12 Screen Height

Screen height is that of an imaginary screen that an aeroplane would just clear in an unbanked attitude with gear extended. For take off it is located at the end of the take off distance required (TODR) and for landing at the beginning of landing distance required (LDR)

Take off screen height is 35' feet for aeroplanes in Performance Class A and 50' for those in Class B

Landing screen height is 50' for both performance classes

In relation to the net take-off flight path, the required 35' vertical distance to clear all obstacles is the minimum vertical distance between the lowest part of the aeroplane and all obstacles within the obstacle corridor.

2.12.1 V_{LOF}

V_{US} is otherwise called V_{LOF}.
Lift-off groundspeed can sometimes be limited by the maximum tyre speed.

$$V_{LOF} \geq \begin{array}{ll} 1.1\,V_{MU} & \text{all engines} \\ 1.05\,V_{MU} & \text{one engine inop} \end{array}$$

The data given for the take-off run and the take-off distance are based upon rotation being initiated at the correct speed. Rotating too early causes additional induced drag thereby reducing the acceleration and increasing the ground run. Rotation too late also increases the ground run but climb capability is good.

Both early and late rotation increase take off distance (TOD)

Rotating too early is the worst scenario since ground run increases and climb gradient decreases. A certain margin is built into the regulations. These require that the take off distance with one engine failed using a rotation speed 5 KT below the correct speed does not exceed the corresponding take off distance using the correct rotation speed.

CRANFIELD AVIATION TRAINING SCHOOL LTD. PART-FCL ATO N° 276
CATS INNOVATION CENTRE, LUTON, Bedfordshire LU2 8DL U.K.   www.catsaviation.com

2-12   Performance

2.12.2 Take off tyre speed limit

Every tyre has a speed rating which is in the flight manual which is related to the maximum ground speed for take-off for that type of tyre. V_{LOF} in terms of GS may be limited by the tyre speed. Factors which can make take-off tyre speed critical are:

- Increased mass
- High altitude
- High temperature
- Tailwind
- Power management computers OFF

2.12.3 V_2

V_2 is the speed that an aeroplane in Performance Class A is required to attain at screen height with one engine inoperative. V_2 is defined as the take-off climb speed or speed at 35'.

$$\begin{matrix} 1.1V_{MCA} \\ 1.13\,V_S \end{matrix} \quad \leq \quad V_{2\,MIN} \quad \leq \quad V_2$$

Thus V_2 varies with air density, take off mass and flap setting

V_{MCA} is a fixed speed that does not vary with weight. Stall speed, however, increases with increasing weight. The minimum value of V_2 is determined by V_{MCA} at low weights and by V_S at higher weights.

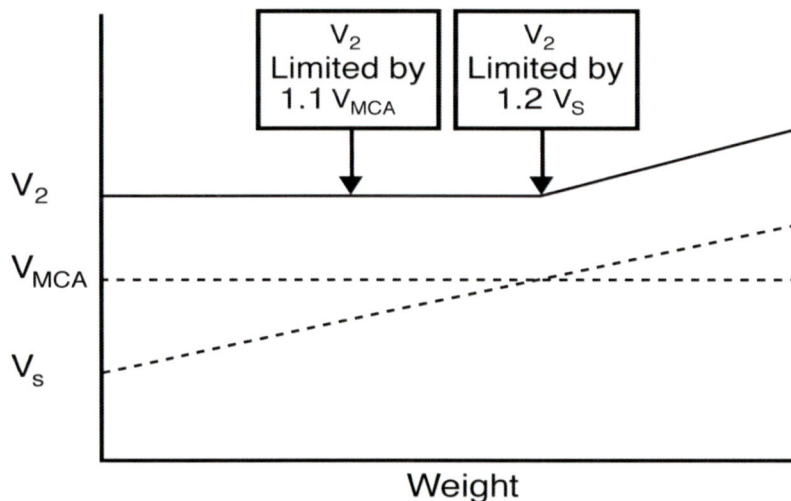

Figure 2.2 The minimum value of V_2 is determined by V_{MCA} at low weights and by V_S at higher weights

2.12.4 V_3 and V_4

With all engines operating, it is assumed that the aeroplane achieves steady initial climb speed, V_3, at screen height and steady take off climb speed, V_4, by 400' gross height.

$$V_3 \geq V_2 + 10 \text{ knots}$$

$$V_4 \geq 1.2\,V_{MCA}$$

V_2 does not apply to aeroplanes in Performance Class B. Instead a free air safety speed is defined as the lowest safe speed at screen height.

For single engine aeroplanes in Performance Class B

$$\text{free air safety speed} \ \geq \ 1.2\,V_{S1}$$

For twin engine aeroplanes in Performance Class B

$$\text{free air safety speed} \ \geq \ \begin{array}{l} 1.1\,V_{MC} \\ 1.2\,V_{S1} \end{array}$$

or a safe speed for a single engine aeroplane to land, and for a twin engine aeroplane to land or continue, allowing for the effects of turbulence and failure of the critical engine

2.13 Increased V₂ take off

An increased V_2 take off enables higher take off mass, or better climb gradients, when climb limited, or obstacle limited, take off mass is below field length limited take off mass, that is, when there exists a large excess of available field length over that required.

To improve climb performance, a higher V_2, equating to V_X, and consequently a higher $V_2/\,V_S$ ratio, is selected in order to obtain more excess thrust. This higher V_2 speed is obtained by accelerating to a higher V_R. The runway limited mass must therefore be reduced.

The optimum $V_2/\,V_S$ ratio is that which gives a field length limited take off mass equal to the climb limited, or obstacle limited, take off mass

2.14 Factors affecting take-off

	Take-off distance	V_{MCG}	V_{MC}	V_1	V_R	V_{LOF}	V_2	Initial Climb performance	V_X	V_Y
Increased altitude	↑	↓	↓	↑	↑	↑	↓	↓		
Increased temperature	↑	↓	↓	↑	↑	↑	↓	↓		
Decreased pressure	↑							↓		
High humidity	↑							↓		
Increased mass	↑			↑	↑	↑	↑	↓	↑	↑
Upslope	↑			↑						
Headwind	↓			↑						
Take-off Flap	↓			↓	↓	↓	↓	↓	↓	↓
TODA > ASDA				↓						
ASDA > TODA				↑						
A/C packs off	↓	↑	↑							
Engine anti-ice on	↑	↑	↑	↑	↑					
PMC off	↑									
Antiskid inoperative				↓						

Table 2.1 Factors affecting take off (TODA: Take-Off Distance Available, ASDA: Accelerate Stop Distance Available, A/C: Air-Conditioning, PMC: Power Management Computer

2.14.1 Mass

Since force, that is engine thrust, is equal to mass times acceleration, a greater mass will result in a slower acceleration, and a longer take off run will be required. In addition, the weight of the aeroplane on the ground, that is its mass times acceleration due to gravity, is entirely supported by the landing gear. A greater weight on the wheels increases friction during the take off run, so again reducing acceleration and extending the take off run.

With increased weight, the stall speed increases. Since the lift-off speed is related to the stall speed, any increase in stall speed must mean an increase in lift-off speed, and a longer take off distance is thus required.

The climb gradient of an aeroplane is inversely proportional to the weight. The climb performance therefore decreases with increasing mass. The increased lift necessary also means more induced drag, which further reduces the climb performance.

2.14.2 Wind

In a headwind take-off, the aeroplane reaches V_{LOF} at a lower groundspeed and a shorter take-off run is required. Thereafter, relative to the ground, a headwind increases the climb gradient whereas a tailwind decreases the climb gradient. Field length and obstacle clearance calculations include correction for not more than 50% of headwind and not less than 150% of tailwind. This is to allow for variations in the reported winds during take-off. A crosswind affects aeroplane controllability. In a strong crosswind, the upwind wing tends to rise in the initial phase of the take-off. There is also a tendency for the aeroplane to drift to the downwind edge of the runway. A take-off crosswind limit is established for all aeroplanes.

2.14.3 Air density

Dynamic pressure is a function of air density and TAS. If density is reduced, a higher TAS is needed to obtain the necessary lift for the same IAS. As a consequence, a longer take off distance is also required. Decreased pressure or increased temperature reduce air density which increase the required take off distance. Air density also affects the power or thrust of an engine. The effect of reduced air density on the power plant output depends on the type of power plant. For normally aspirated reciprocating engines (like those fitted in most single engine piston aeroplanes) the brake horsepower delivered varies with air density. Aeroplanes equipped with this type of engine have their take off distance further increased due to the decrease in take off power with decreasing pressure and increasing temperature.

2.14.4 Supercharging and turbocharging

Supercharged and turbocharged engines are able to deliver full rated power even if the air density decreases. Therefore, aeroplanes equipped with this type of engine normally do not suffer from decreased take off performance due to reduced take off power as density decreases.

2.14.5 Flat rated engines

Turbine engines are usually flat rated up to a temperature of about 30°C at sea level. Flat rated means that up to this temperature the maximum thrust, or maximum torque for turboprop engines, is constant. Above this temperature the output starts to decrease.

> As altitude increases flat rating temperature decreases

CRANFIELD AVIATION TRAINING SCHOOL LTD. PART-FCL ATO N° 276
CATS INNOVATION CENTRE, LUTON, Bedfordshire LU2 8DL U.K.   www.catsaviation.com

2-15   Performance

2.14.6 Reduced thrust take off

Although normal take-off thrust is usually lower than the maximum usable thrust, an additional reduction in thrust increases engine life and reduces noise. Even in the case of engine failure, take-off performance is often much better than necessary. Where the take off mass is lower than the performance limited take-off mass, a reduced take off thrust may be calculated. The constant thrust reduction method was the first to be used. Initially up to 10% thrust reduction was allowed but later on this limit was increased to 25%. Modern engines are usually certified for several different thrust levels for take-off. Any available constant certified rating may be used on both dry and contaminated runways provided that the take-off mass is below the maximum take-off mass for that rating.

The assumed temperature is the latest and best method for derating. The thrust setting is obtained by calculating the maximum allowed temperature for take-off from that runway at actual take off mass. This assumed temperature, is then used to find the corresponding thrust setting for the take-off. The thrust reduction is limited to 25% of the maximum take-off thrust. In the case of engine failure after take off, the one engine-out performance requirements are always satisfied, but go around thrust may be selected for better one engine-out climb performance. The method is not applied where the runway is contaminated. De-icing and anti-icing must not be in use. All EPR gauges, anti-skid systems, thrust reversers and PMC must be operative.

2.14.7 Runway surface and condition

The rolling resistance is the resistance exerted by the tyres when rolling on the runway. The rolling resistance is usually assumed to be proportional to the net downward load, or wheel load, exerted by the aeroplane on the landing gear. The wheel load is equal to the weight, W, minus the lift, L. It is expressed as: Rolling resistance $= \mu_R (W - L)$, where μ_R is a coefficient of rolling resistance that is usually taken to be about 0.025 for a concrete runway. This coefficient depends to some extent on the forward speed, on the inflation and on other characteristics of the tyres. The exact value of the coefficient is not very important in normal conditions because the rolling resistance is usually very small in comparison to the thrust. An important exception occurs when the runway is covered with snow or slush, or in the case of grass fields. These conditions cause a large increase in the coefficient of rolling resistance, which in turn significantly increases the length of the take-off run required.

Performance Class B aeroplanes require a safety factor of 1.2 to be applied to take off distance (TOD) for dry grass up to 20 cm long and 1.3 for wet grass

The runway surface affects not only the aeroplane's acceleration capability but also its stopping capability. This is of primary importance on landing as well as on take off in the case of an aborted take off. Some of the deceleration force is obtained from aerodynamic braking and reverse thrust, the rest is from the use of wheel brakes such that: Deceleration by wheel brakes $= \mu_B (W - L)$, where μ_B is a friction coefficient and is a measure of the braking condition of the runway. The runway braking condition is reported when the runway is contaminated by snow, slush or standing water. The higher the friction coefficient, the better the braking condition of the runway. If there is standing water on the runway the field length limited take-off mass will be decreased.

Measured coefficient	Estimated braking action	Code
0.40 and above	Good	5
0.39 to 0.36	Medium to good	4
0.35 to 0.30	Medium	3
0.29 to 0.26	Medium to poor	2
0.25 and below	Poor	1

Table 2.2 Braking coefficients

2.14.8 Runway slope

A downslope will allow the aeroplane to accelerate faster and will therefore decrease the take-off run. An upslope will make it more difficult for the aeroplane to accelerate, and the take off run will therefore be longer. For aeroplanes in Performance Class A JAR OPS 1.490(c)(4) requires that an operator must take account of runway slope in the direction of take-off when determining maximum permitted take-off mass.

> For aeroplanes in Performance Class B AMC OPS 1.530(c)(5) requires that take off distance (TOD) be increased by a safety factor of 5% for each 1% of up slope

A downslope decreases the take-off speed V_1 because a component of the aeroplane weight is acting in the direction of the thrust.

2.14.9 Runway bearing strength

The bearing strength of a runway has no effect on take-off performance but may limit take-off mass or prohibit an aeroplane from using the runway, and is therefore reported by the aerodrome authority. ICAO Annex 14 describes a system in which Aircraft Classification Number (ACN) is compared with Pavement Classification Number (PCN). For restricted use of the pavement: ACN must be less than or equal to PCN.

$$ACN \leq PCN$$

Overload operations up to 50% may be permitted at the discretion of the aerodrome authority, and above 50% in an emergency only. Information is reported using the following codes:

PCN number	Zero upwards
Pavement type	R Rigid
	F Flexible
Pavement sub-grade category	A High
	B Medium
	C Low
	D Ultra-low
Maximum authorized tyre pressure	W High, no limit
	X Medium, maximum 1.50 MPa
	Y Low, maximum 1.00 MPa
	Z Very low, maximum 0.50 MPa
Pavement evaluation method	T Technical evaluation
	U Experience of aircraft

2.14.10   High lift devices

The ratio of lift to drag is an aerodynamic factor describing airfoil efficiency:

$$\text{Airfoil efficiency} = \frac{C_L}{C_D}$$

where C_L and C_D are the coefficients of lift and drag respectively

The use of flaps and slats can modify the performance of an aeroplane by increasing the maximum lift of the wings, thereby lowering the stall speed and the lift-off speed. Reduction of the lift-off speed reduces the length of the take off run because a shorter distance is needed to accelerate to the lower speed. The use of high lift devices allows a higher take-off mass for a given ground run.

CRANFIELD AVIATION TRAINING SCHOOL LTD. PART-FCL ATO N° 276
CATS CATS INNOVATION CENTRE, LUTON, Bedfordshire LU2 8DL U.K.   www.catsaviation.com

2-17

Performance

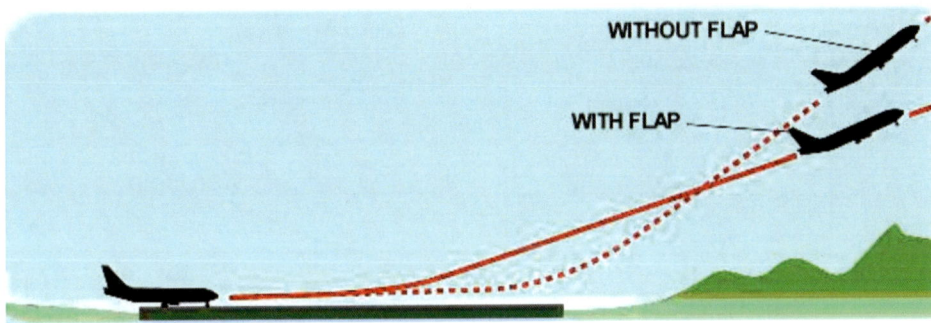

Figure 2.3 Large flap settings increase drag considerably, resulting in much less excess thrust

The selection of a low flap setting for take-off is more likely with a high field elevation, distant obstacles in the climb-out path, long runway and a high ambient temperature. Generally, only moderate flap settings are used for take-off because large flap settings give little additional reduction in stall speed but increase drag considerably. Using a higher take-off flap setting up to the optimum increases the field length limited take-off mass but decreases the climb limited take-off mass.

Example:
Take-off performance data, for the ambient conditions, show the following limitations with flap 15° selected: runway limiting mass: 5500 kg obstacle limiting mass: 4500 kg estimated take-off mass is 5000kg What will be the effect of reducing flap setting for take-off to 5°
The runway limiting mass decreases (in other words less mass can be carried) because less lift is produced thereby increasing the lift-off speed The obstacle limiting mass is increased (in other words more mass can be carried) because there is now less drag in the climb out

Climb gradient is proportional to excess thrust such that: $$\text{Climb gradient} \quad (\%) \quad = \quad \frac{\text{thrust} \; - \; \text{drag}}{\text{weight}} \; \times \; 100$$

Climb gradient, being proportional to excess thrust, is reduced when flaps are selected. The use of flaps to depart from a short runway may therefore adversely affect the ability to clear obstacles or to meet any climb requirement. If there are obstacles in the climb out area, the optimum flap setting depends on the height of these obstacles and their distance from the runway.

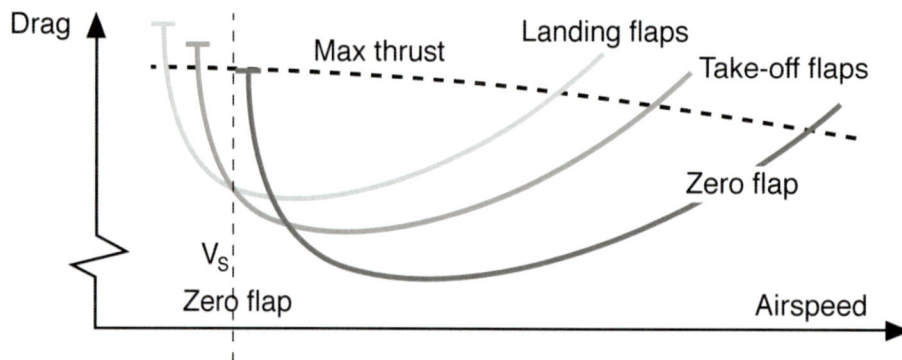

Figure 2.4 Thrust available (broken line or Max thrust) and thrust required, or Drag, for various flap settings plotted against equivalent airspeed (EAS), showing that excess thrust, that is thrust available minus thrust required, and therefore climb gradient, is reduced when flaps are selected. Selection of flap reduces V_S and V_{MD}

2.14.11   Aircraft systems

On turbine aeroplanes, compressor bleed air is often used for air conditioning and de-icing. In the temperature range where the engine is flat rated the use of bleed air does not affect engine thrust because it is the thrust, or torque, which is flat rated and not the power developed in the turbine. In the range where the engine is not flat rated the turbine limits the thrust that may be produced, so if some of the turbine output is used to produce bleed air, thrust from the engine is reduced.

2.15 Definitions of take off distances

2.15.1 Accelerate stop distance ASD

Accelerate stop distance is the distance to accelerate from brake release point to V_1 and then to brake safely to a halt.

2.15.2 Accelerate stop distance available ASDA

Accelerate stop distance available is the distance declared by an aerodrome authority as available to accelerate from brake release point to V_1 and then to brake safely to a halt.

$$ASDA = TORA + stopway$$

2.15.3 Accelerate stop distance required ASDR

For aeroplanes in Performance Class A, the longest of the distances during which:

a.   With all engines operating on a dry runway, the aeroplane accelerates until 2 s after it reaches V_1, at which point the engines are reduced and the aeroplane decelerates to a full stop. The delay is the decision time for the pilot to react and disengage any automatic thrust control system

CRANFIELD AVIATION TRAINING SCHOOL LTD. PART-FCL ATO N° 276
CATS INNOVATION CENTRE, LUTON, Bedfordshire LU2 8DL U.K.   www.catsaviation.com

2-19   Performance

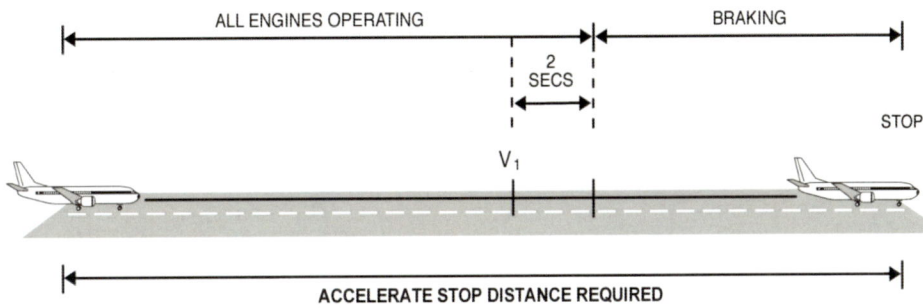
Figure 1.5 ASDR all engines dry runway

b.   With all engines operating on a wet runway, as for (a) except acceleration continues to V_{STOP} + 2 s.

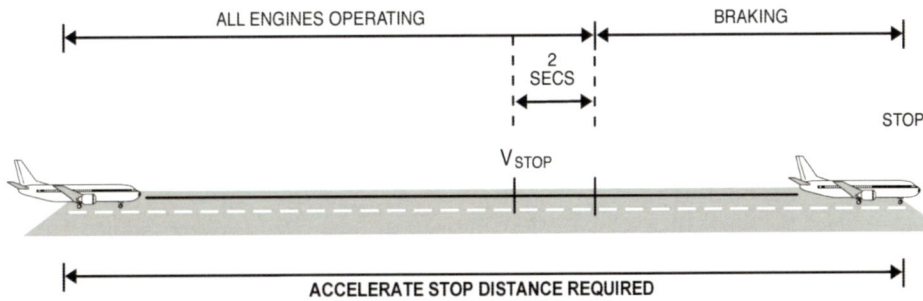
Figure 1.6 ASDR all engines wet runway

c.   On a dry runway the aeroplane accelerates from brake release point to V_{EF} at which point the critical engine fails. The aeroplane continues to accelerate until it reaches V_1, the interval between V_{EF} and V_1 being called the recognition time and being approximately 2 s. The aeroplane continues to accelerate for another 2 s, the decision time, before the engines are reduced and brakes applied. From this point the aeroplane starts to decelerate and comes to a full stop.

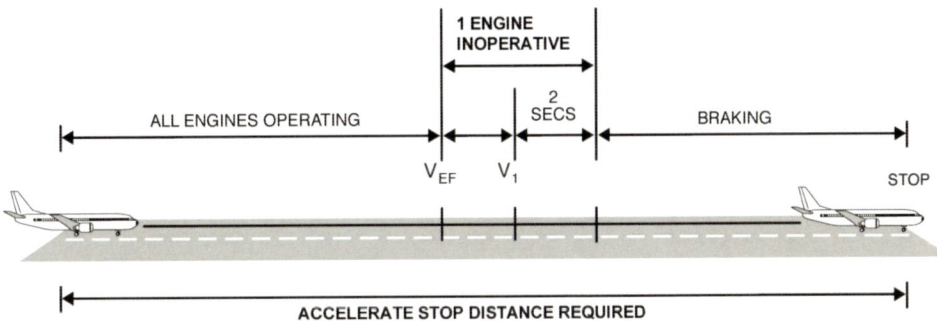
Figure 1.7 ASDR engine failure dry runway

d.   On a wet runway, as for (c) except V_1 is replaced by V_{STOP}

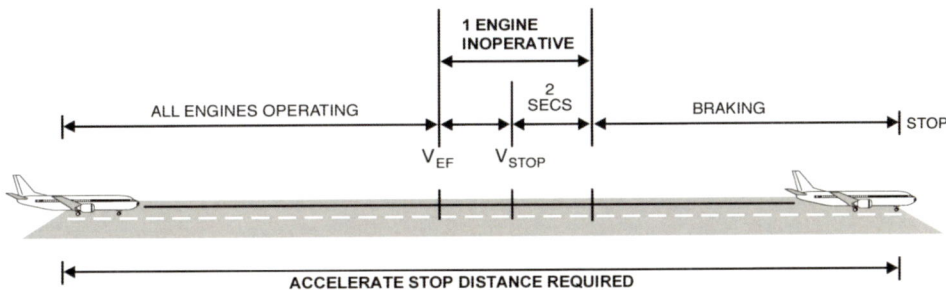
Figure 1.8 ASDR engine failure wet runway

CRANFIELD AVIATION TRAINING SCHOOL LTD. PART-FCL ATO N° 276
CATS INNOVATION CENTRE, LUTON, Bedfordshire LU2 8DL U.K.

www.catsaviation.com

Performance

2-20

$$\text{ASDR} \leq \text{ASDA}$$

The distance to reach V_1 or V_{STOP} will be the longest with the critical engine failed. The distance covered in the 2 seconds after V_1 or V_{STOP} is the longest with all engines operating.

When determining ASDR, means other than wheel brakes may be used provided they are safe and reliable, that consistent results can be obtained under normal operating conditions and that exceptional skill is not required to control the aeroplane. The use of thrust reversers has normally not been found to satisfy these requirements, thus ASDRs given in the Aircraft Flight Manual are usually not based upon the use of thrust reversers

2.15.4 Clearway

Clearway is a rectangular area beyond the end of TORA, in the direction of the extended centreline and with a semi-width of 75 m, limited by the first non-frangible (solid) obstacle liable to endanger an aeroplane in the take off climb.

$$\text{Clearway} \leq \frac{\text{TORA}}{2}$$

The length of a clearway may be included in the take-off distance available.

2.15.5 Stopway

An obstacle-free rectangular area beyond the end of TORA with the same width as the associated runway and over which an aeroplane may safely roll in an emergency without structural damage. Braking coefficient, strength and slope are similar to those of the runway

2.15.6 Take off distance TOD

Take-off distance is the distance to accelerate from brake release point to V_R and then climb to screen height.

For aeroplanes in Performance Class B	
where no stopway or clearway exists	1.25 TOD $\leq$ TORA i.e. TOD $\leq$ 80% of TORA
where a stopway or clearway exists	TOD $\leq$ TORA 1.15 TOD $\leq$ TODA, i.e. TOD $\leq$ 87% TODA 1.3 TOD $\leq$ ASDA, i.e. TOD $\leq$ 77% of ASDA

2.15.7 Take off distance available TODA

The distance declared by an aerodrome authority as available to take-off and reach screen height. TODA is limited by the first non-frangible (solid) obstacle liable to endanger an aeroplane in the take off climb or by the length of clearway.

$$\text{TODA} = \text{TORA} + \text{clearway}$$

2.15.8 Take off distance required TODR

The take-off performance requirements for transport category aeroplanes are based upon failure of critical engine or all engines operating which ever gives the largest take off distance

According to JAR 25 for an aeroplane in Performance Class A, the longest of:

a.   With all engines operating on a dry runway, 1.15 times the distance between brake release point and screen height.

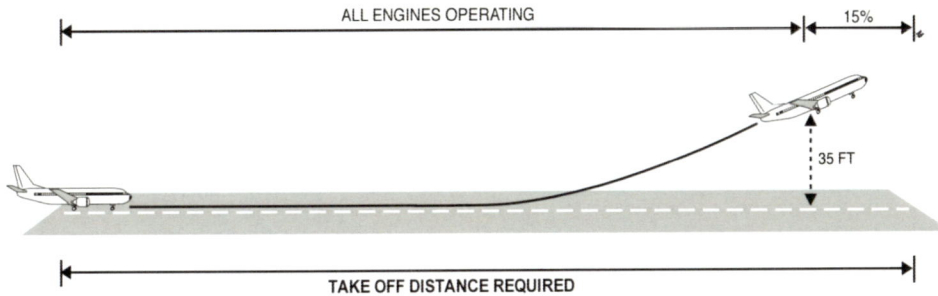

Figure 1.9 TODR all engines dry runway

b.   As for (a), except on a wet runway.

c.   On a dry runway, from brake release point to the point where the aeroplane reaches a height of 35' and V_2, with critical engine failure having occurred at V_{EF}

d.   On a wet runway, from brake release point to the point where the aeroplane reaches a height of 15', with critical engine failure having occurred at V_{EF} corresponding to V_{GO} and achieved in a manner consistent with reaching V_2 by a height of 35'.

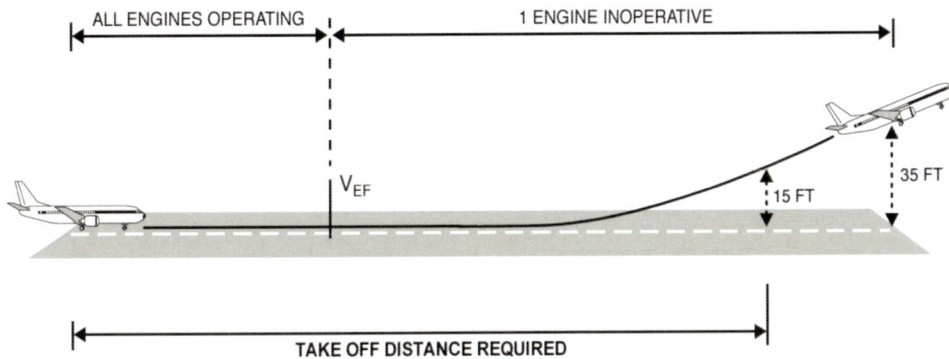

Figure 1.10 TODR engine failure wet runway

Example:

During the certification flight testing of a twin engine turbojet aeroplane, the real take-off distances are equal to:

1500 m with all engines running
1650 m with failure of critical engine at V1,

What will be the take-off distance used for the certification file?
Multiply the 1500 m with all engines running by 1.15
1500 m x 1.15 = 1725 m
1725 m is longer than the 1650 m with failure of critical engine at V1
Take the longest distance as the answer: 1725 m

For a four engine aeroplane the all engines operating distance is usually the longest. For a two engine aeroplane the distance in the case of engine failure is usually the longest.

TODR ≤ TODA

Where a clearway exists not less than half of the airborne distance between the lift off point and the 35' point must be within TORA. Thus, even with an extremely long clearway, not all of it may be used to climb to 35'.

2.15.9 Take off run TOR

The distance to accelerate from brake release point to V_{LOF}

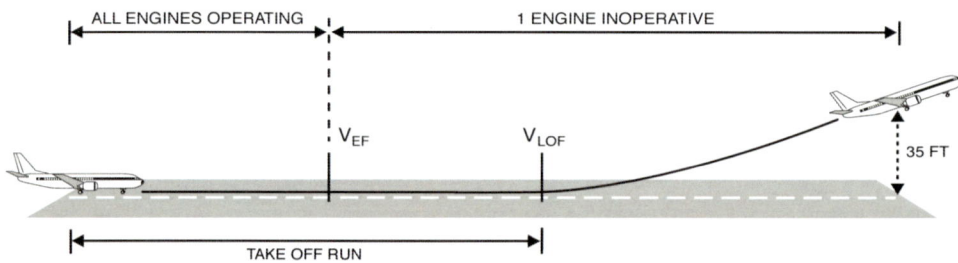

Figure 1.11 Take off run (TOR)

2.15.10   Take off run available TORA

The distance declared by an aerodrome authority as available in the direction of take off having uniform braking coefficient, slope and bearing strength and being free of non-frangible (solid) obstacles.

2.15.11   Take off run required TORR

Where no clearway exists TORR is less limiting than ASDR and therefore need not be considered. Where a clearway exists, for an aeroplane in Performance Class A according to JAR-OPS 1, TORR is the longest of:

a.   With all engines operating, 1.15 times the distance between brake release point to the point equidistant between the lift off point and screen height.

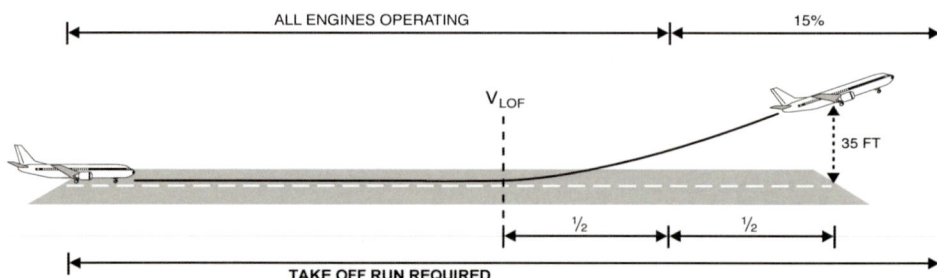

Figure 1.12 TORR all engines

b.   On a dry runway with critical engine failure occurring at V_{EF}, from brake release point to a point equidistant between V_{LOF} and screen height.

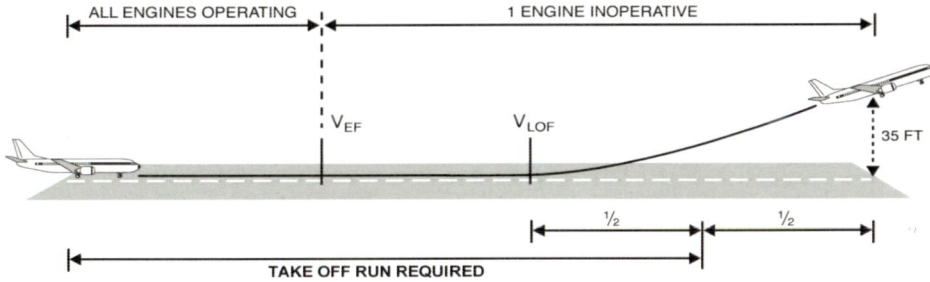

Figure 1.13 TORR engine failure dry runway

c.   On a wet runway with critical engine failure occurring at V_{EF} corresponding to V_{GO}, from brake release point to V_{LOF}

TORR $\leq$ TORA

The gross take off distance is contained within 87% of TORA (100 / 1.15)

2.16 Balanced field take off

Decision speed V_1 must lie within a speed range between V_{MCG} and V_R. How large this range is depends on how great the take-off mass is with respect to the field length limited take-off mass (FLL TOM). A low V_1 will allow a relatively short ASD since less distance will be needed to accelerate to the decision speed giving a relatively short acceleration distance. Also, less kinetic energy has to be dissipated during braking, giving a shorter stopping distance. A low V_1 will however give a relatively long take off distance because acceleration is assumed to occur with one engine failed from V_1 to V_R.

A low V_1 will allow a relatively short ASD and a relatively long TOD

The advantage of a balanced field length condition is that the minimum required field length is available in the event of an engine failure.

MTOM is achieved by selecting a V_1 which has TOD and ASD of equal length

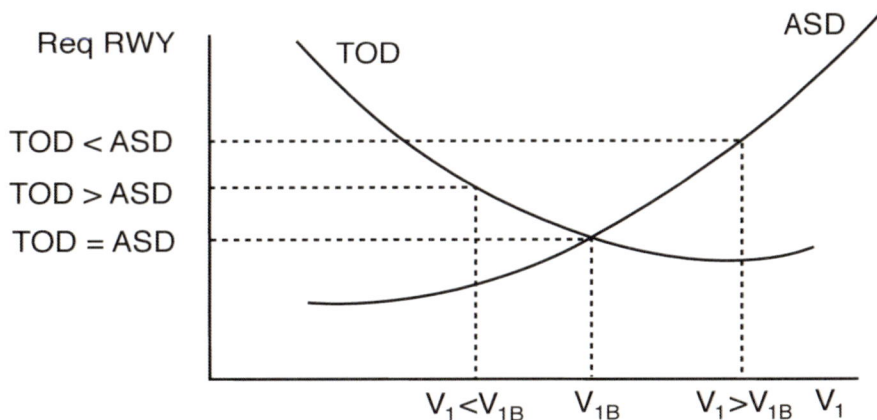

Figure 2.14 For a balanced field take off TOD equals ASD and V_1 is called V_{1B}. As V_1 increases ASD increases and TOD decreases. If $V_1 < V_{1B}$ then TOD > ASD and if $V_1 > V_{1B}$ then TOD < ASD

A balanced field length is defined as: ASDA = TODA

2.17 Wet runway take-off

For take-off from a wet runway V_{STOP} defines the highest decision speed from which the aeroplane can be stopped within ASDA. V_{GO} defines the lowest decision speed from which a continued take off is possible within the take off distance available. As V_{STOP} is less than V_{GO}, if an engine failure occurs between V_{STOP} and V_{GO} the speed is too high to abort the take off and too low to reach screen height at the usual point. Thus a V_1 at V_{STOP}, rather than at V_1 for a dry runway, leads to a longer take off distance for a given mass. This may, however, be compensated for by a reduction in screen height to 15' at the end of TODA. On a wet runway some of the margin in the take off distance has thus been sacrificed in order to avoid a severe reduction in take off mass. The margin in the aborted take off case has not been reduced - it must be possible to stop on the remaining runway should the take off be rejected at V_1. Sometimes the lower screen height required on a wet runway leads to a higher allowable take off mass than from a dry runway, however, JAR-OPS 1 prohibits a take off mass higher than that calculated for a dry runway. Additionally, the all engines TODR must still meet the requirement for a dry runway, that is, 1.15 times the take off distance to 35'. TODR is then the longer of the one engine out wet runway TODR and the all engines dry runway TODR.

2.18 Contaminated runway take-off

Contamination causes reduced braking friction, increased rolling resistance and, in the case of standing water, a risk of aquaplaning. The provision of flight test data for these conditions is not required but criteria exist upon which guidance materials must be based. The required distances are calculated in the same manner as for take off from wet runways. Calculations assume critical engine failure at V_1. Take-off using variable or reduced thrust may be prohibited, as may take-off where the contaminant depth may cause spray impingement damage.

CRANFIELD AVIATION TRAINING SCHOOL LTD. PART-FCL ATO N° 276
CATS INNOVATION CENTRE, LUTON, Bedfordshire LU2 8DL U.K.   www.catsaviation.com

2-25

Performance

Self Assessment Test 02

1   What is measured performance?
A)   The average performance of an aeroplane or group of aeroplanes undergoing test by an acceptable method under specified conditions
B)   The average performance that a fleet of aircraft should achieve if satisfactorily maintained and flown in accordance with the techniques described in the Flight Manual
C)   The gross performance diminished to allow for various contingencies that cannot be accounted for operationally
D)   The best performance that an aircraft can achieve

2   What is net performance?
A)   The best performance that an aircraft can achieve
B)   The average performance that a fleet of aircraft should achieve if satisfactorily maintained and flown in accordance with the techniques described in the Flight Manual
C)   The average performance of an aeroplane or group of aeroplanes undergoing test by an acceptable method under specified conditions
D)   The gross performance diminished to allow for various contingencies that cannot be accounted for operationally

3   According to JAR-OPS, an operator shall ensure when no stopway or clearway is available for a Performance B aircraft that:
A)   The unfactored take off distance does not exceed when multiplied by a factor of 1.25 the take off run available
B)   The unfactored take off distance does not exceed when multiplied by a factor of 1.43 the take off run available
C)   The longer of A and B above
D)   None of the above

4   How is gradient or slope calculated?
A)   Change in horizontal distance / height
B)   Change in height / horizontal distance
C)   Change in height - horizontal distance
D)   Horizontal distance - horizontal distance

5   What is V_S?
A)   Safety speed
B)   Stall speed
C)   Steady climb speed
D)   Safe descent speed

6   What is V_{S0}?
A)   Stall speed
B)   Stall speed with flap in landing configuration
C)   Stall speed with flap in take off landing configuration
D)   Safety speed with flap in landing configuration

7   What is V_Y?
A)   The speed used to attain the maximum angle of climb
B)   The speed used to attain the minimum rate of climb
C)   The speed used to attain the maximum rate of climb
D)   The speed used to attain the minimum angle of climb

8   Which of the following is most correct for an aeroplane in a climb?
A)   Lift is less than weight
B)   Thrust must exceed drag if speed is to be maintained
C)   Drag is greater than weight
D)   Lift is greater than weight

9   Flying horizontally in a turn:
A)   Less power is required than in level flight
B)   More power is required than in level flight
C)   The same power is required
D)   More or less power may be required depending on which side of the drag curve the aeroplane is sitting

10   With the centre of gravity on the forward limit, the stalling speed would be:
A)   Independent of the centre of gravity position
B)   Lower than with the centre of gravity on the aft limit
C)   Higher than with the centre of gravity on the aft limit
D)   The same as with the centre of gravity on the aft limit

11   Changing the take-off flap setting from flap 15° to flap 5° will normally result in:
A)   a better climb and an equal take-off distance
B)   a longer take-off distance and a better climb
C)   a shorter take-off distance and a better climb
D)   a shorter take-off distance and an equal climb

12   The result of a higher flap setting up to the optimum at take-off is
A)   a longer take-off run
B)   a shorter ground roll
C)   a higher V_1
D)   an increased acceleration

13   Which of the following speeds can be limited by the maximum tyre speed?
A)   Lift-off TAS
B)   Lift-off IAS
C)   Lift-off EAS
D)   Lift-off groundspeed

14   A higher pressure altitude at ISA temperature
A)   decreases the take-off distance
B)   increases the climb limited take-off mass
C)   has no influence on the allowed take-off mass
D)   decreases the field length limited take-off mass

15   A 0.5 cm layer of wet snow contaminates a runway. The take-off is nevertheless authorised by the flight manual for a light twin.
      The take-off distance in relation to a dry runway is likely to be:
A)   unchanged
B)   increased
C)   decreased
D)   very significantly decreased

16 On a dry runway the accelerate stop distance is increased
A) by a lower take-off mass because the aeroplane accelerates faster to V_1
B) by low outside air temperature
C) by headwind
D) by uphill slope

17 The stopway is an area which allows an increase only in:
A) the accelerate-stop distance available
B) the landing distance available
C) the take-off run available
D) the take-off distance available

18 Which of the following distances will increase if you increase V_1?
A) Accelerate Stop Distance
B) Take-off run
C) Take-off distance
D) All Engine Take-off distance

19 How does runway slope affect allowable take-off mass, assuming other factors remain constant and not limiting?
A) A downhill slope decreases allowable take-off mass
B) An uphill slope increases take-off mass
C) A downhill slope increases allowable take-off mass.
D) Allowable take-off mass is not affected by runway slope

20 Which of the following represents the maximum value for V_1 assuming max tyre speed and max brake energy speed are not limiting?
A) V_{MCA}
B) V_R
C) V_2
D) V_{REF}

21 What will be the influence on the aeroplane performance if aerodrome pressure altitude is increased?
A) It will increase the take-off distance
B) It will increase the accelerate stop distance available
C) It will increase the take-off distance available
D) It will decrease the take-off distance

22 Which of the following represents the minimum for V_1?
A) V_{LOF}
B) V_{MCG}
C) V_{MU}
D) V_R

23 Which statement is correct?
A) V_R is the lowest climb speed after engine failure
B) In case of engine failure below V_R the take-off should be aborted
C) V_R is the speed at which rotation should be initiated
D) V_R is the lowest speed for directional control in case of engine failure

CRANFIELD AVIATION TRAINING SCHOOL LTD. PART-FCL ATO N° 276
CATS INNOVATION CENTRE, LUTON, Bedfordshire LU2 8DL U.K.   www.catsaviation.com

CATS

2-28   Performance

24   Which statement is correct?
A) V_R must not be less than 1.1 V_{MCA} and not less than V_1
B) V_R must not be less than V_{MCA} and not less than 1.05 V_1
C) V_R must not be less than 1.05 V_{MCA} and not less than V_1
D) V_R must not be less than 1.05 V_{MCA} and not less than 1.1 V_1

25   During certification flight testing on a four engine turbojet aeroplane the actual take-off distances measured are:
     - 3000 m with failure of the critical engine recognised at V_1
     - 2500 m with all engines operating and all other factors being equal
A)   3000 m
B)   2875 m
C)   3450 m
D)   2555 m

26   What is the result of a large take-off flap setting compared to a small take-off flap setting on required TOD and FLL TOM?
A)   Decreased TOD required and decreased FLL TOM
B)   Increased TOD required and increased FLL TOM
C)   Increased TOD required and decreased FLL TOM
D)   Decreased TOD required and increased FLL TOM

27   V_2 has to be equal to or higher than:
A)   1.1 V_{MCA}
B)   1.1 V_{S0}
C)   1.15 V_R
D)   1.15 V_{MCG}

Self Assessment Test 02 Answers

1	A
2	D
3	A
4	B
5	B
6	B
7	C
8	A
9	B
10	C
11	B
12	B
13	D
14	D
15	B
16	D
17	A
18	A
19	C
20	B
21	A
22	B
23	C
24	C
25	A
26	D
27	A

CRANFIELD AVIATION TRAINING SCHOOL LTD. PART-FCL ATO N° 276
CATS INNOVATION CENTRE, LUTON, Bedfordshire LU2 8DL U.K.

www.catsaviation.com

Performance

2-30

CHAPTER 3
The Net Take–off Flight Path

3.1   The climb segments

The profile path of an aeroplane after it reaches the end of TODR, plotted using gross performance data, is called the gross take off flight path. The profile path of an aeroplane plotted from the same point using net performance data is called the net take off flight path. The net take off flight path is always below the gross take off flight path. Both end at a horizontal distance from the end of TODR at which the net take off flight path is 1500' net height above reference zero.

Reference zero is an imaginary plane passing through a point 35' or 50' vertically beneath the aeroplane at the end of TODR

JAR 25 divides the initial airborne phase into four segments, each with a specified aeroplane configuration and speed. The critical engine is assumed to have failed.

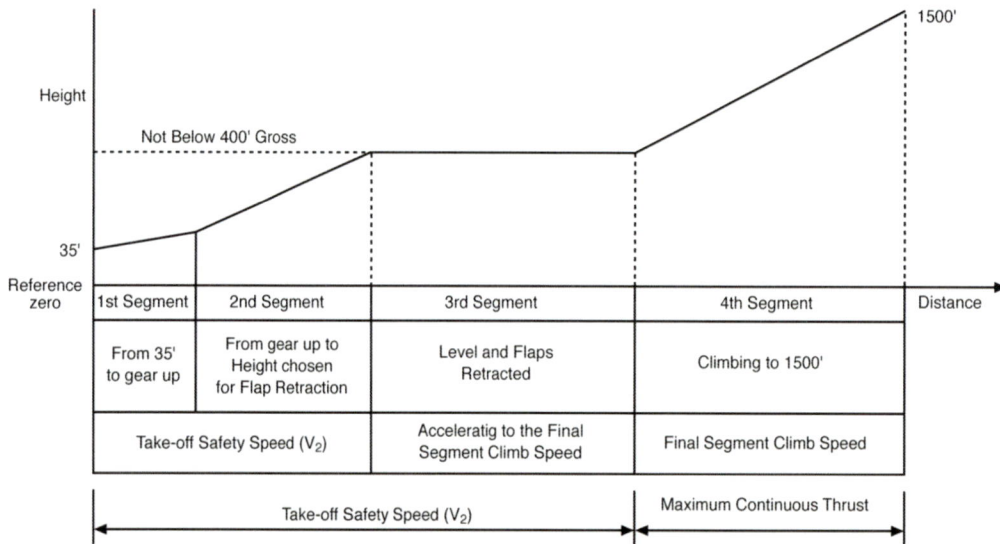

Figure 3.1 The climb segments

The first climb segment is the initial airborne phase with the aeroplane accelerating from lift off speed to V_2. The remaining engines are at take-off thrust, the flaps in the take-off position and the gear is down. Gear up is selected when positive rate of climb is confirmed and the first segment ends when the gear is up.

Take-off thrust (a certified rating) and V_2 are maintained in the second segment to obtain the best possible climb gradient. Flaps reduce the climb gradient but are not retracted because the speed would have to be increased before the retraction, resulting in a loss in climb performance. The second segment extends to a minimum of 400' above ground level but may extend higher if this is necessary for terrain clearance.

The third segment, called the transition or acceleration segment, is used to change the aeroplane from the take off configuration to the clean configuration. As the aeroplane accelerates, usually in level flight, the flaps and slats are retracted at scheduled speeds. The minimum speed to which the aeroplane should be accelerated is 1.25 V_S, but for practical reasons it is accelerated to speed for best engine-out rate of climb which is called clean speed. At the end of the segment, thrust is reduced to maximum continuous thrust (a certified rating) on the operating engines.

In the fourth segment, the operating engines are at maximum continuous thrust. The speed is a minimum of $1.25\ V_S$, but clean speed is generally used. The segment ends when transition to the en route altitude is reached.

3.2   Climb requirements

JAR 25 specifies the climb gradients that the aeroplane must achieve along the take off path. These are set to ensure that the aeroplane has a certain climb and manoeuvring ability in the initial airborne phase - they have nothing to do with obstacle clearance and must be met even if the initial climb takes place over water. Obstacle clearance may require higher climb gradients.

Number of engines	Minimum climb gradient		
	1st segment	2nd segment	3rd and final segments
2	Positive	2.4%	1.2%
3	0.3%	2.7%	1.5%
4	0.5%	3.0%	1.7%

Table 3.1 Climb gradient requirements in the take off flight path

according to JAR 25

Gross gradients are the gradients that the aeroplane is capable of achieving with one engine inoperative. Wind has no effect on the gradients requirements. The requirements are seldom limiting for the allowable take-off mass except at high airport altitudes and temperatures. The limiting case is generally the second segment for which performance charts are included in the Aircraft Flight Manual.

For aeroplanes in Performance Class B JAR-OPS 1 states that, with all engines operating, the climb gradient from 50' to the assumed engine failure height, at the point where visual reference for the purposes of avoiding obstacles is expected to be lost, is equal to the average gradient during climb and transition to the en route configuration multiplied by 0.77, equating to a distance travelled multiplied by 1.3.

> For aeroplanes in Performance Class B
>
> all engines take off climb gradient $\geq$ 4%

From the assumed engine failure height to 1500' above reference zero the climb gradient is assumed to be that shown in the Aircraft Flight Manual, which must be measurably positive at 400' and not less than 0.75% at 1500'.

3.3   Obstacle requirements

The net take off flight path must clear all obstacles within the obstacle accountability area vertically by a minimum of 35', and by 50' when banked more than 15°.

> In relation to the net take-off flight path, the required 35' vertical distance to clear all obstacles is the minimum vertical distance between the lowest part of the aeroplane and all obstacles within the obstacle domain

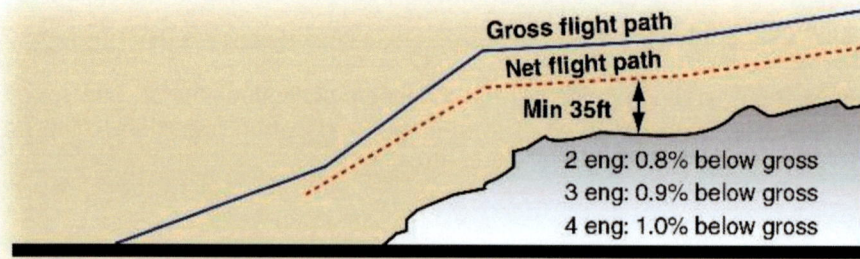

Figure 3.2 The net take off flight path is based on the net gradient, which is the gross gradient reduced by a factor depending on the number of engines

3.3.1 Obstacle Accountability Area

The obstacle accountability area begins at the end of TODA, or at the end of TOD if a turn is scheduled before the end of TODA, and ends when the aeroplane reaches a net height of 1500' above reference zero. Obstacles lying outside a lateral distance of 90 m, or 60 m plus ½ the wingspan if the wingspan is less than 60 m, plus one eighth, (x 0.125) the distance from the end of TODA or TOD, are not considered. The width of the obstacle accountability area is limited where track changes are less than 15°, and subject to the pilot being able to maintain navigational accuracy. Track changes are not permitted below the larger of ½ the wingspan or 50', and bank angles are limited to 15° below 400' and 25° thereafter.

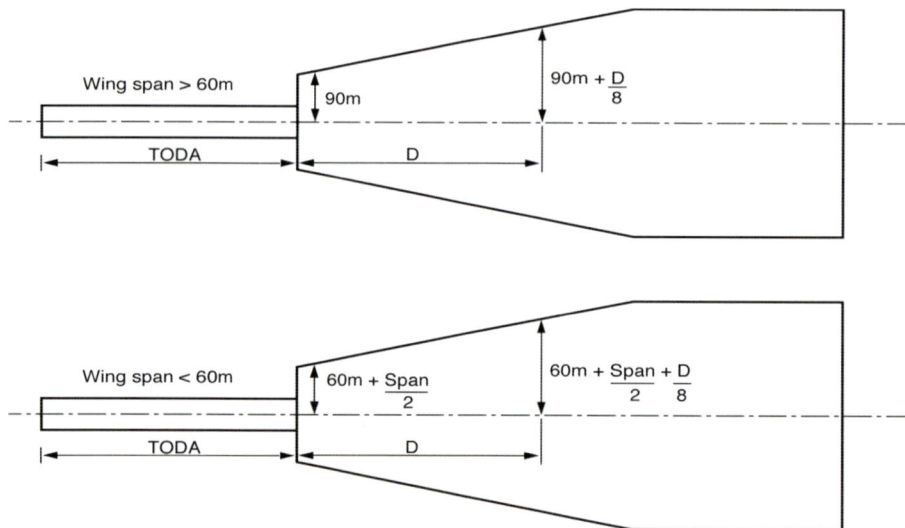

Figure 3.3 The obstacle accountability area

Bank angle is limited in the net take off flight path because induced drag increases as more lift is required, reducing excess thrust and therefore climb gradient. V_S also increases with increasing bank angle, giving less margin to the stall for a given speed.

3.4 All engines speed restriction

During a normal take off a speed higher than V_2 will be obtained at 35'. The speed in the second segment is usually limited to V_2 + 10 KT unless maximum take off attitude is reached. This restriction is imposed to ensure that the all engines flight path does not fall below the one-engine failed flight path. Faster speeds could result in insufficient obstacle clearance.

3.5   Noise abatement departure procedures (NADPs)

ICAO Document 8168 PANS-OPS, which contains information on instrument departure and approach procedures, suggests two methods for departure from noise sensitive areas:

3.5.1   NADP1 first part noise relief

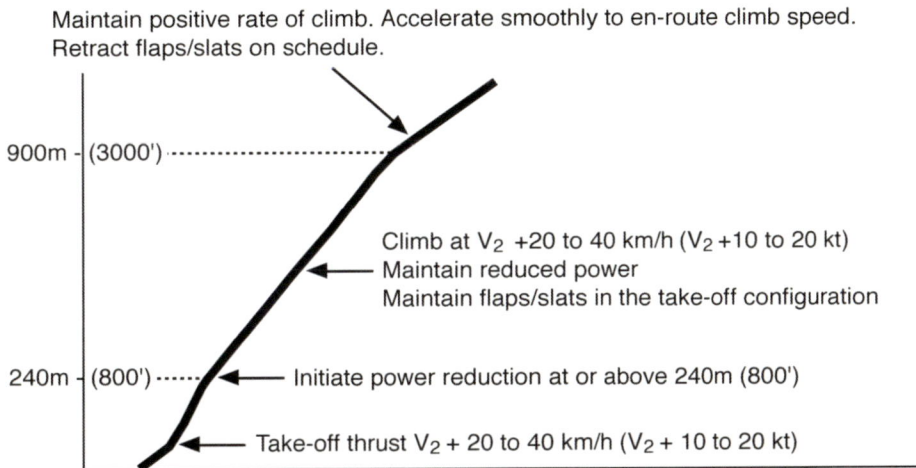

Maintain positive rate of climb. Accelerate smoothly to en-route climb speed.
Retract flaps/slats on schedule.

900m – (3000') ·······

Climb at V_2 +20 to 40 km/h (V_2 +10 to 20 kt)
Maintain reduced power
Maintain flaps/slats in the take-off configuration

240m – (800') ······   Initiate power reduction at or above 240m (800')

Take-off thrust V_2 + 20 to 40 km/h (V_2 + 10 to 20 kt)

Figure 3.4 NADP1 Acceleration segment for flap/slat reduction at maximum prescribed height

This is a normal second segment all-engines operating procedure up to a prescribed minimum height above the runway surface of 800'. Thereafter, instead of maintaining take off thrust and accelerating, the thrust is reduced to climb thrust and the speed kept at V_2+10 to 20 KT up to 3000' above the runway, with *no flaps retraction*. At 3000' the aeroplane is accelerated smoothly with flap retraction on schedule.

3.5.2   NADP2 latter part noise relief

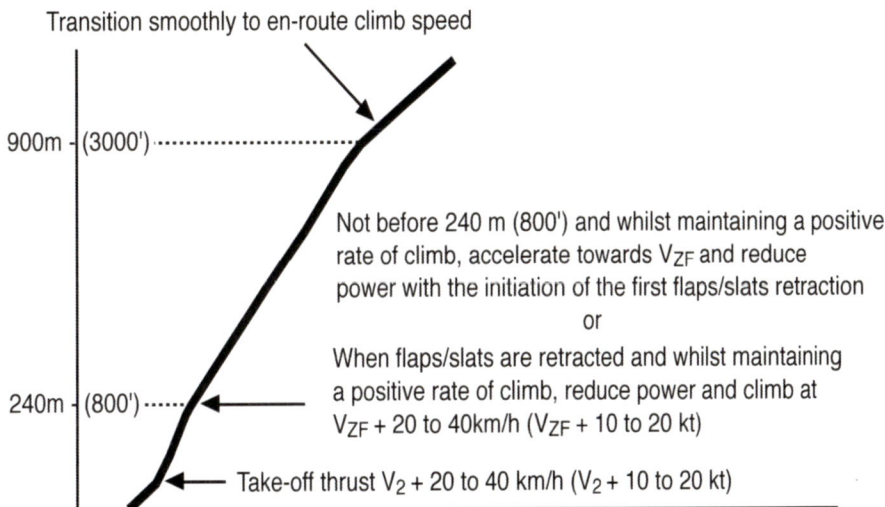

Transition smoothly to en-route climb speed

900m – (3000') ·······

Not before 240 m (800') and whilst maintaining a positive
rate of climb, accelerate towards V_{ZF} and reduce
power with the initiation of the first flaps/slats retraction
or
When flaps/slats are retracted and whilst maintaining
a positive rate of climb, reduce power and climb at
V_{ZF} + 20 to 40km/h (V_{ZF} + 10 to 20 kt)

240m – (800') ·····

Take-off thrust V_2 + 20 to 40 km/h (V_2 + 10 to 20 kt)

Figure 3.5 NADP2 Acceleration segment for flap/slat reduction before maximum prescribed height

The second segment configuration is flown up to 800' above the runway surface with a speed of V_2+10 to 20 KT and take off thrust. At 800', acceleration is begun maintaining a positive rate of climb. Flaps are retracted at zero flap safe manoeuvring speed, V_{ZF}, and thrust is reduced. This speed plus 10 knots is maintained up to 3000'. At this height the aeroplane is accelerated smoothly to en route climb speed.

CRANFIELD AVIATION TRAINING SCHOOL LTD. PART-FCL ATO N° 276
CATS INNOVATION CENTRE, LUTON, Bedfordshire LU2 8DL U.K.   www.catsaviation.com

3-4   Performance

Self Assessment Test 03

1   At which minimum height will the second climb segment end?
A)   35' above ground
B)   When gear retraction is completed
C)   1500' above field elevation
D)   400' above field elevation

2   The requirements with regard to take-off flight path and the climb segments are only specified for:
A)   the failure of the critical engine on a multi-engines aeroplane
B)   the failure of two engines on a multi-engined aeroplane
C)   2 engined aeroplane
D)   the failure of any engine on a multi-engined aeroplane

3   An operator shall ensure that the net take-off flight path clears all obstacles. The half-width of the obstacle-corridor at the distance D from the end of the TODA is at least:
A)   90m + 0.125D
B)   0.125D
C)   -90m + 1.125D
D)   90m + D/0.125

CRANFIELD AVIATION TRAINING SCHOOL LTD. PART-FCL ATO N° 276
CATS INNOVATION CENTRE, LUTON, Bedfordshire LU2 8DL U.K.

www.catsaviation.com

3-5

Performance

Self Assessment Test 03 Answers

1	D
2	A
3	A

CRANFIELD AVIATION TRAINING SCHOOL LTD. PART-FCL ATO N° 276
CATS INNOVATION CENTRE, LUTON, Bedfordshire LU2 8DL U.K.

www.catsaviation.com

Performance

3-6

CHAPTER 4
Forces and Speeds in the Climb

4.1 Climb gradient

The climb gradient is defined as the ratio of the increase of altitude to horizontal air distance expressed as a percentage

4.2 Resolving vectors

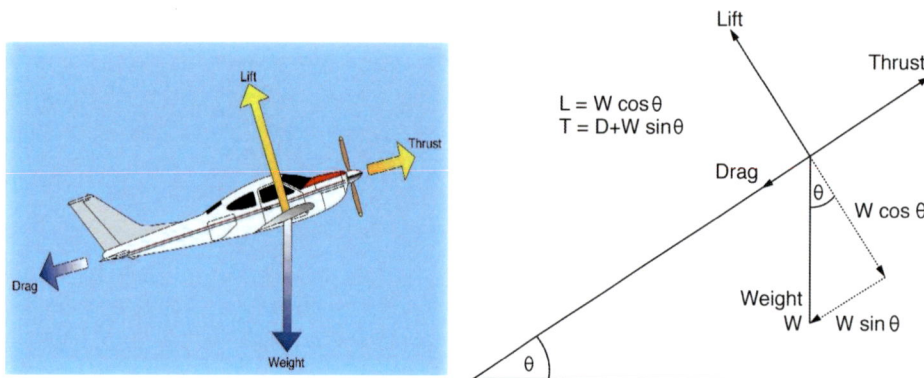

$$L = W \cos\theta$$
$$T = D + W \sin\theta$$

Figure 4.1 Forces acting on an aeroplane in a steady unaccelerated climb are lift, normal to the flight path, thrust and drag, parallel to the flight path, and weight vertically downwards

Any acceleration in climb with a constant power setting decreases the rate of climb and the angle of climb. There is a speed for the best rate of climb and if you are flying faster than this you must have pitched the nose down. If the nose is pitched down the angle of climb will be reduced.

In an unaccelerated climb thrust equals drag plus the downhill component of weight in the flight path direction

In an aeroplane in a steady unaccelerated climb, the angle between the flight path and the horizontal, the climb angle, is indicated by θ (theta). The weight can be resolved into two vectors, one opposite to and countered by lift:

$$W \cos\theta$$

and the other parallel to the flight path in the direction of drag:

$$W \sin\theta$$

The climb angle of the aeroplane, θ, is given by:

$$\sin\theta = \frac{\text{thrust - drag}}{\text{weight}}$$

For small climb angles the unaccelerated percentage climb gradient may be expressed approximately by:

Climb Gradient = ((Thrust - Drag)/Weight) x 100

Climb Gradient = (ROC / TAS)

Example:

A climb gradient required is 3.0%. For an aircraft maintaining 100 KT TAS, still air, this climb gradient corresponds to a rate of climb of approximately:

Climb Gradient = (ROC / TAS)
3.0 % = (ROC / 100 KT)
ROC = 3.0 % x 100
ROC = 300 fpm

4.3   Best angle climb speed V_X and best rate of climb speed V_Y

4.3.1 V_X

V_X	is the speed for best angle of climb
	represents the maximum excess of thrust
	is $\leq V_y$

Climb gradient (angle) is proportional to excess thrust, therefore the speed for maximum climb gradient, or maximum angle of climb, V_X, occurs where excess thrust is greatest. The thrust from turbofan and turbojet engines can be considered independent of speed. V_X is therefore the same as V_{MD} for a jet aeroplane.

CRANFIELD AVIATION TRAINING SCHOOL LTD. PART-FCL ATO N° 276
CATS INNOVATION CENTRE, LUTON, Bedfordshire LU2 8DL U.K.   www.catsaviation.com

CATS

4-2   Performance

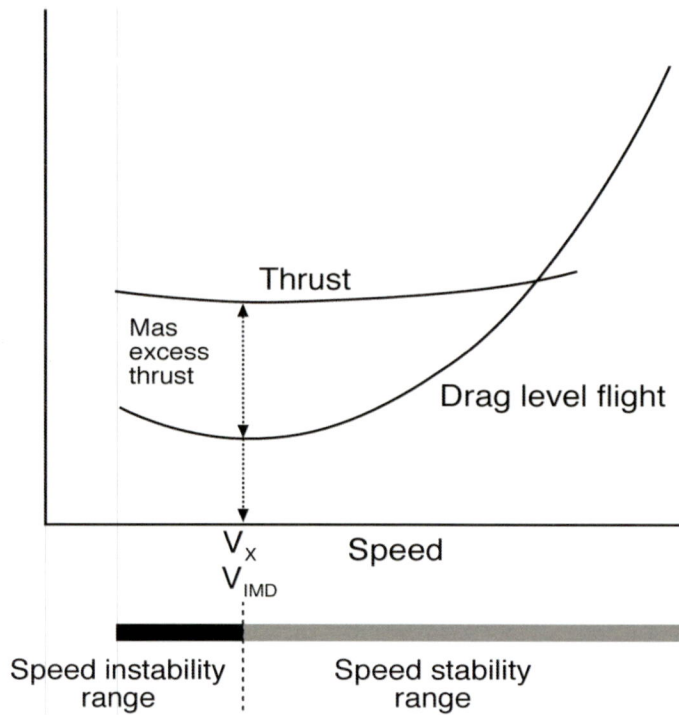

Figure 4.2 Thrust available for a turbojet aircraft is independent of speed thus V_X is equal to V_{IMD}. At a speed above that for minimum drag the aeroplane is speed stable since drag increases with speed. At a speed below V_{MD}, however, the aeroplane is speed unstable, demanding more active control from the pilot. This is the case at V_X, especially in a propeller aeroplane where V_X is below V_{MD}

Propeller aeroplanes, however, have a thrust curve that varies with speed, and V_X is therefore generally a slightly lower speed than minimum drag speed.

> The most important aspect of being on the 'backside of the power curve' is that the speed is unstable

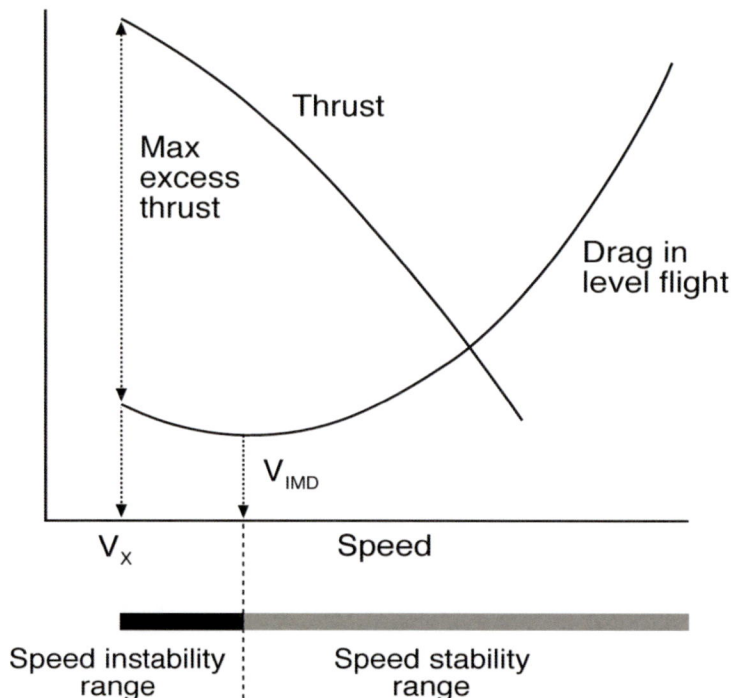

Figure 4.3 Thrust available for a piston-propeller aircraft varies with speed

The use of V_X is limited to the end of the take off phase and the beginning of the climb phase when a steep climb angle is required to clear obstacles. After that, a high rate of climb is more practical to reach a flight level as quickly as possible. V_X is a speed close to the stall speed and close to, or in, the speed unstable range.

> Power is defined as the rate of doing work, and may be expressed as:
>
> $$Power = thrust \times TAS$$

Applying the above equation, a power required curve may be developed from the thrust required curve by multiplying the thrust required at each point on the curve by the TAS at that point. Power available can be developed from thrust available in the same way.

> Rate of climb is proportional to excess power such that:
>
> $$Rate\ of\ climb = \frac{power\ available\ -\ power\ required}{weight}$$

> Rate of climb is approximately climb gradient times true airspeed divided by 100

4.4 Best rate of climb speed V_Y

V_y	is the speed for best rate of climb
	represents the maximum excess of power

The speed at which excess power is greatest is therefore the speed for best rate of climb, called V_Y. On this new curve V_{MD} occurs at the tangent to the curve of a straight line from the origin.

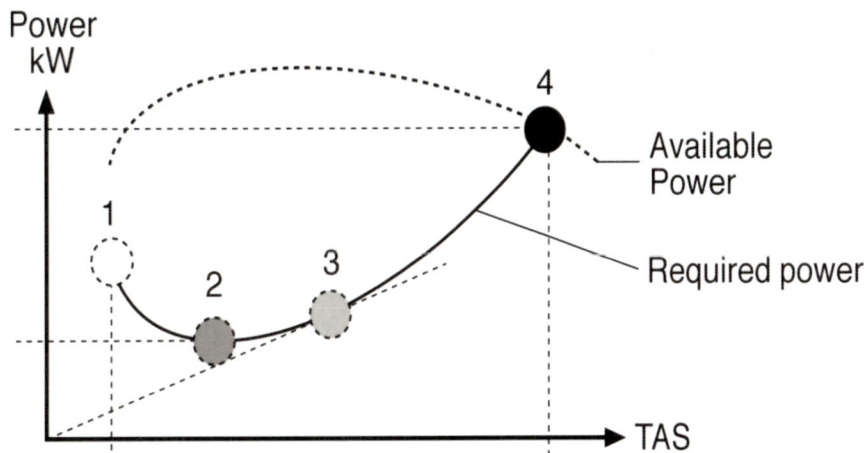

Figure 4.4 Point 1 is V_S, point 2 is V_{MP} and the speed for minimum rate of descent, point 3 is V_{MD}, best L:D and speed for best gliding distance and point 4 is the maximum speed

For a jet engine that has constant thrust with speed, the power available curve appears as a straight line drawn from the origin. For a piston or turboprop aeroplane, the power available is relatively high in the low speed regime however the curve flattens out at higher speeds.

CRANFIELD AVIATION TRAINING SCHOOL LTD. PART-FCL ATO N° 276
CATS INNOVATION CENTRE, LUTON, Bedfordshire LU2 8DL U.K.   www.catsaviation.com

4-4

Performance

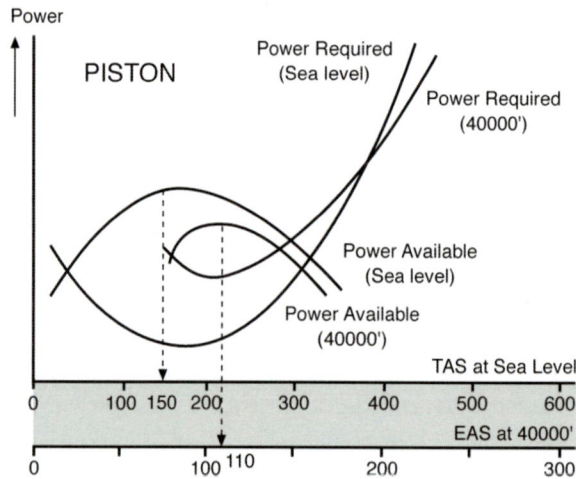

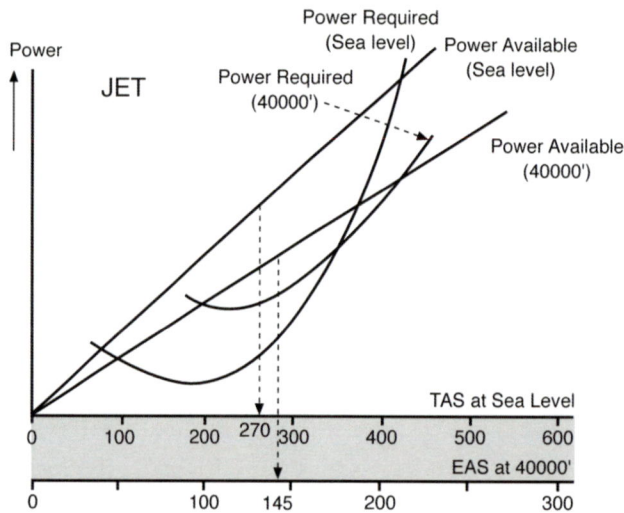

Figure 4.5 Power available versus power required for piston propeller and jet aeroplanes

V_Y is not normally used as an operational climb speed. A cruise climb speed is adopted instead. This higher climb speed is a compromise to get the optimum balance between groundspeed and rate of climb - the object is to reach the destination as fast as possible with minimum fuel consumption.

As long as an aeroplane is in a positive climb Vx is always below Vy.

4.5 The effects of altitude, flap and mass on climb performance

4.5.1 Effect of altitude on climb performance

With increasing altitude when plotted against TAS, the power required curve moves up (less thrust is generated due to the lower air density so more power is required) and to the right (IAS held constant in low altitude climbs results in an increasing TAS) while the power available curve moves down (less thrust available due to the lower air density). Rate of climb therefore decreases due to the loss of excess power. However, with increasing altitude the speed (Vy) for best rate of climb increases when measured as a TAS. Generally an aeroplane's climb schedule requires a climb at constant IAS, rather than at constant TAS, until a particular Mach number is reached. A typical jet cruise climb is performed at 300 KT IAS until reaching

CRANFIELD AVIATION TRAINING SCHOOL LTD. PART-FCL ATO N° 276
CATS INNOVATION CENTRE, LUTON, Bedfordshire LU2 8DL U.K.

CATS

www.catsaviation.com

4-5

Performance

Mach 0.75 at around 27000'. Since IAS is a function of dynamic pressure, $\frac{1}{2}\rho V^2$, TAS, V, increases with altitude, that is, with reducing density ρ, if IAS is held constant.

	IAS	TAS	angle of attack	pitch	climb gradient
climb at constant IAS	constant	↑	constant	↓	↓
climb at constant Mach	↓	↓	↑	↑	↑
descent at constant Mach	↑	↑	↓	↓	↑
descent at constant IAS	constant	↓	constant	constant	constant

Table 4.1 Acceleration while climbing at constant IAS causes a reduction in climb gradient and therefore in climb performance. In order to maintain optimum climb performance the Aircraft Flight Manual for a piston-propeller aeroplane may specify a reducing climb IAS with altitude. For jet aeroplanes climbing at constant Mach above the crossover altitude, climb performance instead improves with altitude

Variation in rate of climb with change in speed can be shown in a polar diagram showing rate of climb against speed. V_X may also be shown on this diagram, being the speed corresponding to the tangent to the curve of a straight line from the origin. Any acceleration in climb, with a constant power setting decreases the rate of climb and the angle of climb.

In a polar diagram showing the effects of altitude on climb rate it can be seen that indicated speed for maximum rate of climb decreases slowly with increasing altitude. Indicated speed for maximum angle of climb, however, increases with increasing altitude, and coincides with speed for maximum rate of climb at absolute ceiling. However, as V_X is used only during take off and at low altitude, it is normally defined as a single speed. For practical reasons V_Y is also usually indicated as an average value.

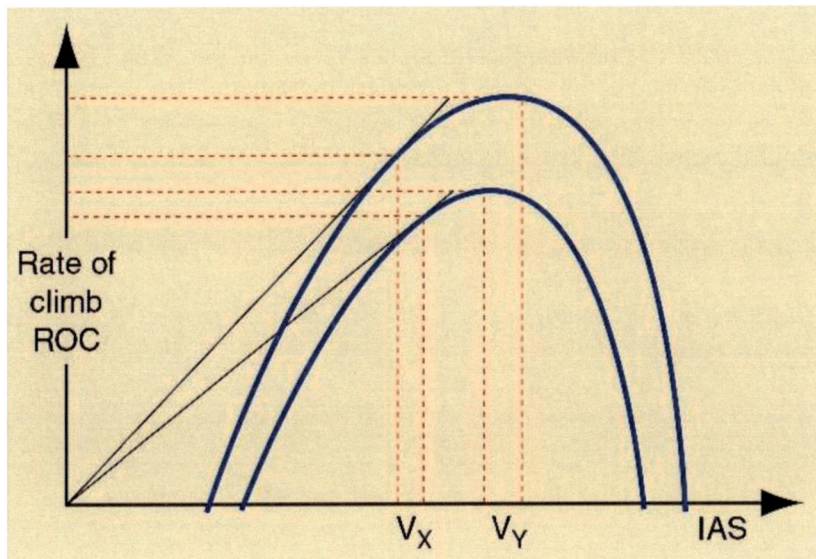

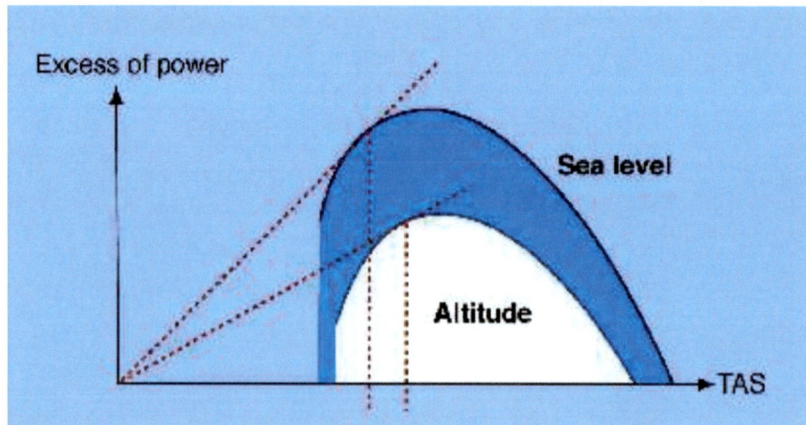

Figure 4.7 With increasing altitude the curve of excess power, and therefore V_Y, shifts to the left when plotted against IAS but to the right when plotted against TAS. On both graphs V_X increases with altitude

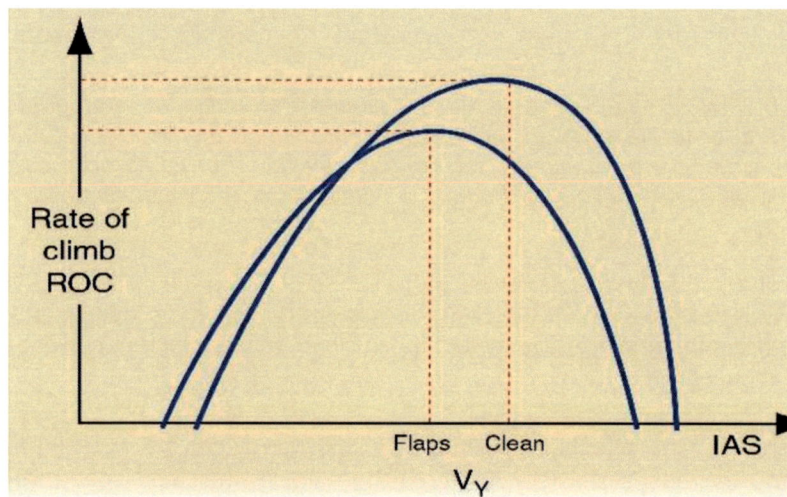

Figure 4.8 With increased flap setting climb performance and V_Y decrease

4.6   The effect mass on climb performance

Increased mass requires more lift and therefore produces more induced drag. The power required curve therefore moves up and slightly to the right. As power available is the same, a decrease in climb performance is observed since less excess power is available. Speeds for maximum rate of climb and maximum angle of climb increase with increasing mass.

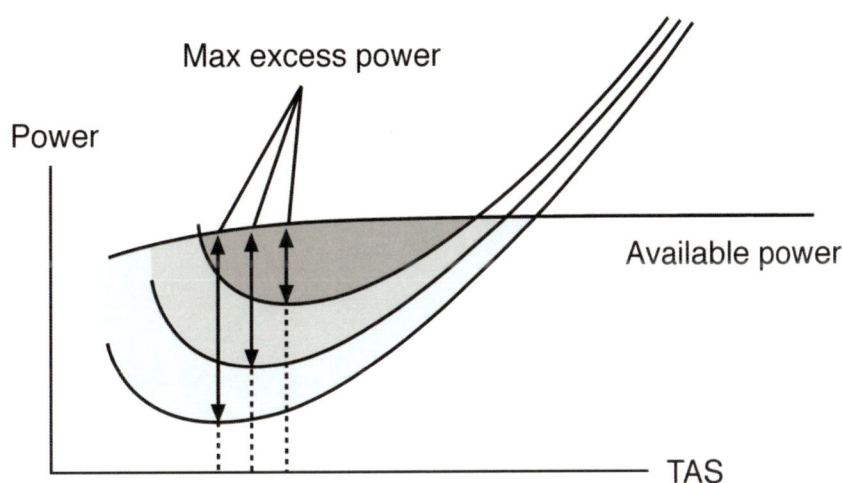

Figure 4.9 V_Y increases with mass

Higher gross mass at the same altitude decreases the angle / gradient and the rate of climb whereas the speeds V_x and V_Y are increased

4.7   Effect of wind on climb performance

A constant headwind decreases the distance travelled over the ground. This increases the angle of the climb flight path and also the climb gradient. However, the maximum climb angle speed stays constant.

A constant headwind component increases the angle of flight path during climb

However, a headwind component increasing with altitude, as compared to zero wind condition, (assuming IAS is constant) has no effect on the rate of climb.

A constant headwind component has no affect on the rate of climb

Wind has no effect on the climb limited take-off mass. Obstacle limited take off mass is however affected by wind.

4.8   Effect of temperature on climb performance

A higher outside air temperature reduces the angle and the rate of climb

4.9   Flight into an inversion

At an inversion, due to inertia, the aeroplane flies into the new air mass with airspeed relative to the air mass it leaves. In case of an increasing headwind or decreasing tailwind above the inversion, the airspeed increases momentarily and so does the rate of climb. When climbing through high altitude wind shear, the airspeed can increase beyond M_{MO}. If the headwind decreases or the tailwind increases above the inversion, the airspeed and rate of climb decrease, leading to a decrease in excess thrust.

4.10 Engine-out climb

Consider a twin engine aeroplane with a maximum rate of climb of 1500 fpm. Following an engine failure power available is reduced by 50%. Power required is unchanged. Best rate of climb speed is now referred

CRANFIELD AVIATION TRAINING SCHOOL LTD. PART-FCL ATO N° 276
CATS INNOVATION CENTRE, LUTON, Bedfordshire LU2 8DL U.K.   www.catsaviation.com

4-8   Performance

to as best single engine rate of climb speed, V_{YSE}, and is slightly less than V_Y. It may be marked on the ASI with a blue line and is therefore sometimes called blue line speed. Maximum rate of climb has reduced to 300 fpm and best single engine angle of climb speed, V_{XSE}, is slightly increased.

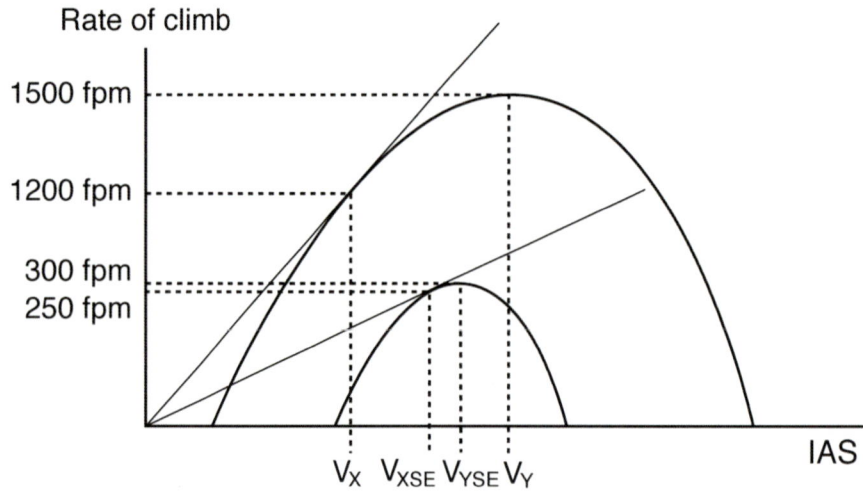

Figure 4.12 $V_{XSE} > V_X$ whereas $V_{YSE} < V_Y$

CRANFIELD AVIATION TRAINING SCHOOL LTD. PART-FCL ATO N° 276

CATS CATS INNOVATION CENTRE, LUTON, Bedfordshire LU2 8DL U.K.

www.catsaviation.com

4-9

Performance

Self Assessment Test 04

1   A headwind component increasing with altitude, as compared to zero wind condition, (assuming IAS is constant):
A)   does not have any effect on the angle of flight path during climb
B)   has no effect on rate of climb
C)   improves angle and rate of climb
D)   decreases angle and rate of climb

2   A higher outside air temperature
A)   increases the angle of climb but decreases the rate of climb
B)   reduces the angle and the rate of climb
C)   does not have any noticeable effect on climb performance
D)   reduces the angle of climb but increases the rate of climb

3   Assuming that the required lift exists, which forces determine an aeroplane's angle of climb?
A)   Weight, drag and thrust
B)   Weight and thrust only
C)   Thrust and drag only
D)   Weight and drag only

4   How does the best angle of climb and best rate of climb vary with increasing altitude?
A)   Best angle of climb increases while best rate of climb decreases
B)   Both increase
C)   Best angle of climb decreases while best rate of climb increases
D)   Both decrease

5   The pilot of a single engine aircraft has completed climb performance calculations. The carriage of an additional passenger will cause the climb performance to be:
A)   Degraded
B)   Unchanged, if a short field take-off is adopted
C)   Improved
D)   Unchanged

6   During climb to the cruising level, a headwind component
A)   decreases the ground distance flown during that climb
B)   increases the amount of fuel for the climb
C)   increases the climb time
D)   decreases the climb time

7   The angle of climb with flaps extended, compared to that with flaps retracted, will normally be:
A)   Increase at moderate flap setting, decrease at large flap setting
B)   Larger
C)   Not change
D)   Smaller

8   What is the influence of the mass on maximum rate of climb (ROC) speed if all other parameters remain constant?
A)   The ROC speed decreases with increasing mass
B)   The ROC and the ROC speed are independant of the mass
C)   The ROC is affected by the mass, but not the ROC speed
D)   The ROC speed increases with increasing mass

CRANFIELD AVIATION TRAINING SCHOOL LTD. PART-FCL ATO N° 276
CATS INNOVATION CENTRE, LUTON, Bedfordshire LU2 8DL U.K.   www.catsaviation.com

4-10   Performance

9   Which of the following provides maximum obstacle clearance during climb?
A)   1.2Vs
B)   The speed, at which the flaps may be selected one position further up
C)   The speed for maximum rate of climb
D)   The speed for maximum climb angle Vx

10   With an true airspeed of 194 KT and a vertical speed of 1000 fpm, the climb gradient is about :
A)   3%
B)   3°
C)   5°
D)   8%

11   Which one of the following is not affected by a tail wind?
A)   the climb limited take-off mass
B)   the field limited take-off mass
C)   the obstacle limited take-off mass
D)   the take-off run

12   The rate of climb is:
A)   the angle of climb x TAS
B)   the downhill component of TAS
C)   The horizontal component of TAS
D)   approximately climb gradient x TAS divided by 100

Self Assessment Test 04 Answers

1	B
2	B
3	A
4	D
5	A
6	A
7	D
8	D
9	D
10	B
11	A
12	D

CHAPTER 5
The Cruise

5.1 Range and endurance

Range is the *distance* that may be flown on a certain amount of fuel

To optimise range, gross fuel flow, that is $\dfrac{\text{fuel flow}}{\text{groundspeed}}$, must be minimised

Endurance is the time that may be flown on a certain amount of fuel

In a given configuration the endurance of a piston-engined aeroplane depends on altitude, speed, mass and fuel on board.

Minimising the work done in overcoming drag, that is flying at the most efficient airframe speed, and minimising the work done in overcoming drag per unit time, would suggest flying at V_{MD} for maximum range and at V_{MP} for maximum endurance. However, the most efficient airframe speed is not necessarily also the most efficient speed at which to operate the aeroplane's engines.

It is interesting to see the differences between the speeds for maximum endurance, V_{ME}, and maximum range, V_{MR}, for piston-propeller and turbojet aircraft.

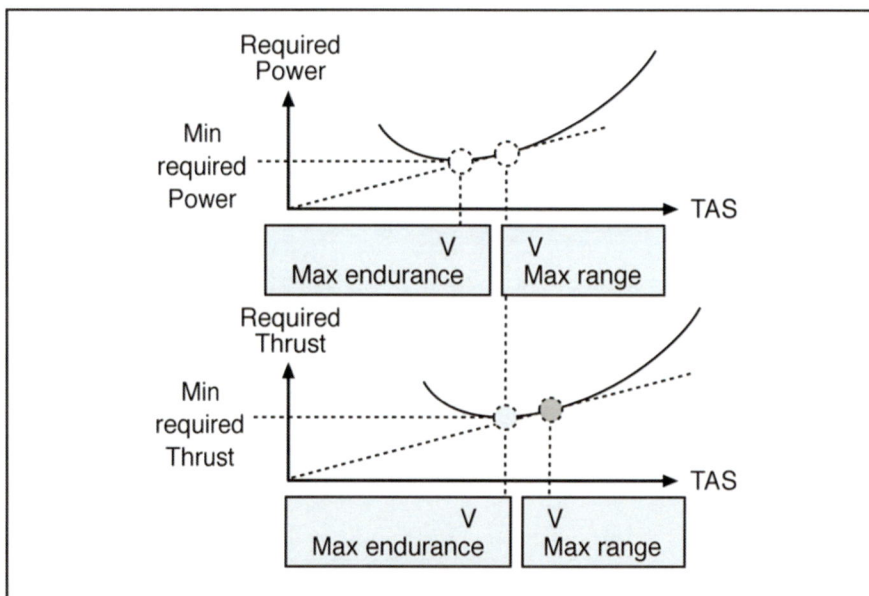

Figure 5.1 Speeds for maximum endurance and maximum range for piston-propeller (top) and turbojet aircraft (bottom)

5.1.1 Piston-propeller aeroplanes

The maximum indicated air speed of a piston engined aeroplane, in level flight, is reached at lower altitudes than in jet aircraft. At higher altitudes a propeller is less efficient because the air is less dense.

For piston engine aeroplanes fuel flow is approximately proportional to power setting

To achieve a low rate of fuel consumption, and thus optimise endurance, power should be minimized for a piston-propeller aeroplane.

For a piston-propeller aeroplane V_{ME} = V_{IMP}

V_{MR} occurs where the ratio between power and speed required is minimum. This point is the tangent to the power required curve of a straight line from the origin.

Since Power required = thrust required × TAS

the ratio of power to speed is equal to thrust required, or drag,

$$\frac{\text{Power required}}{\text{TAS}} = \frac{\text{thrust required} \times \text{TAS}}{\text{TAS}}$$

$$= \text{thrust required}$$

$$= \text{drag}$$

It follows that V_{MR}, which is where the ratio of power to speed is a minimum, is also the speed for minimum drag.

For a piston-propeller aeroplane V_{MR} = V_{MD}

The point at which a tangent out of the origin touches the power required curve is the point where the Lift to Drag ratio is a maximum

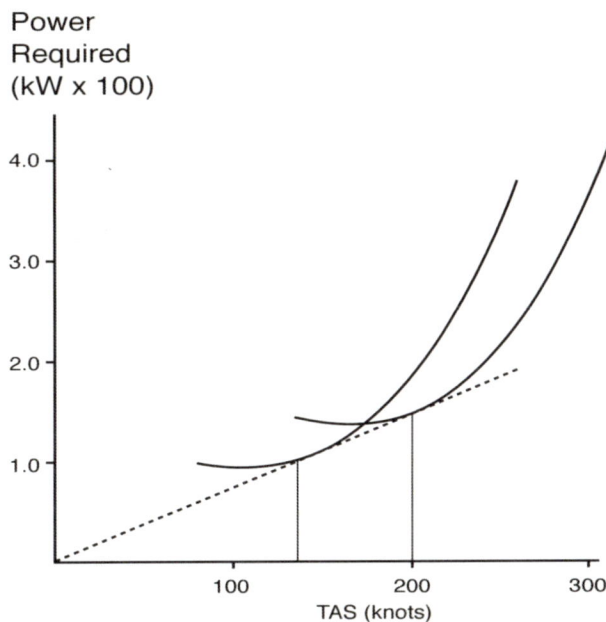

Figure 5.2 TAS for maximum range for piston aeroplanes increases with altitude

Since it is a function of dynamic pressure, $\frac{1}{2}\rho v^2$, at constant IAS, drag remains constant with increasing altitude but TAS increases. Thus, since power required equals drag times TAS, power required increases with altitude. Thus maximum endurance for piston engine aeroplanes decreases with increasing altitude. Note that the tangent to the different power curves is the same, which means that maximum range for piston aeroplanes is independent of altitude.

> IAS for maximum endurance and range is constant with increasing altitude

> TAS for maximum endurance and range increases with increasing altitude

Selecting V_{MR} as the cruising speed for aeroplanes with normally aspirated reciprocating engines is generally not practical because at low altitude the resulting TAS and power loading is low. A more practical speed is one called cruise optimum speed. This is the speed resulting in minimum fuel consumption per speed unit. It is calculated in the same way as V_{MR} was calculated from the power versus speed graph. Cruise optimum speed is the tangent to the thrust required curve of a straight line from the origin and results in a speed about 1.3 times V_{MR}.

5.1.2 Jet aeroplanes

Jets operate at higher altitudes than piston engined aircraft principally because fuel consumption is less in the less dense air. The maximum indicated air speed of a jet aeroplane, in level flight, is reached at higher altitudes than in piston-engined aircraft. At higher altitudes a propeller is less efficient because the air is less dense, whereas a jet can still efficiently operate.

> For jet aeroplanes, fuel flow is approximately proportional to thrust setting

Speed for maximum endurance therefore occurs where thrust required to maintain level flight is minimum and is therefore the same as that for minimum drag.

> For a jet aeroplane V_{ME} = V_{IMD}

Since drag is constant at all altitudes for a given IAS the indicated speed for maximum endurance is independent of altitude. By implication the maximum endurance is itself independent of altitude. In practice, however, fuel consumption decreases slightly with altitude, due to a higher propulsive efficiency at higher TAS (TAS increasing with altitude for a constant IAS) and better efficiency due to higher engine rpm.

V_{MR} for jet aeroplanes occurs at the point where IAS is a maximum for the least amount of drag, that is, where the ratio between thrust required and speed is a minimum. This point is the tangent to the power required curve of a straight line from the origin.
In the same way as IAS for minimum drag is constant with altitude, IAS for maximum range is constant with altitude also. However, since TAS for minimum drag increases with altitude for a constant IAS, maximum range increases with altitude.

5.2 The effect of wind on V_{ME} and V_{MR}

Wind does not affect V_{ME} since the only measured criteria is the flying time possible with a certain amount of fuel. V_{MR}, conversely, is greatly affected by wind because the wind alters ground speed and hence the ground distance flown.

> Wind has no effect on maximum endurance speed

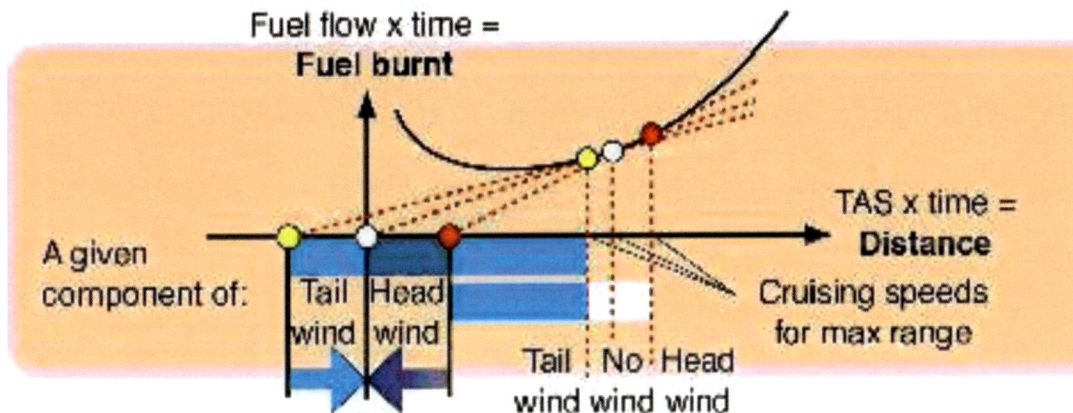

Figure 5.3 A headwind results in a higher V_{MR} and a tailwind in a lower V_{MR}

A headwind increases maximum range speed

To achieve the maximum range over ground with a headwind the airspeed should be higher compared to the speed for maximum range cruise with no wind.

5.3   Hourly consumption

At a given altitude, hourly consumption of a turbojet is directly proportional to aeroplane mass. For example if aeroplane mass decreases by 5% (assuming the engines specific consumption remains unchanged) the hourly consumption is approximately decreased by the same amount of 5%.

5.4   Specific fuel consumption and specific air range

Specific Fuel Consumption (SFC) $= \dfrac{\text{fuel flow (kg hour}^{-1})}{\text{thrust (N)}}$

SFC decreases with decreasing temperature and increasing RPM.

Specific Air Range (SAR) is the still air distance travelled per unit of fuel
$$SAR = \frac{TAS}{drag} \times \frac{1}{SFC}$$
Below M_{CRIT} maximum $\dfrac{TAS}{drag}$ is 1.32 V_{IMD}

For a jet aeroplane, because fuel flow is proportional to thrust, this curve has the same shape as the thrust required curve.

If other factors are unchanged, the fuel mileage (nautical miles per kg) is lower with a forward centre of gravity position.

Positioning the centre of gravity slightly forward of the aft limit reduces induced drag and improves SAR

CRANFIELD AVIATION TRAINING SCHOOL LTD. PART-FCL ATO N° 276
CATS INNOVATION CENTRE, LUTON, Bedfordshire LU2 8DL U.K.   www.catsaviation.com

5-4   Performance

5.5   Maximum range and long range cruise speeds

Consider a graph of SAR against TAS. The curve has its maximum at best SAR. The corresponding speed is called maximum range cruise speed, V_{MRC}. If speed deviates from this flight efficiency will be eroded.

The maximum SARs for different altitudes can be joined with a curve to give the variation of V_{MRC} with altitude. The altitude at which V_{MRC} is greatest is the optimum altitude.

Jet aeroplanes, having relatively high fuel consumption, initially have a high mass and therefore a low initial optimum altitude. As fuel is consumed, mass reduces and higher, more efficient altitudes become available. This procedure is called a cruise climb, and is executed at constant Mach number, angle of attack and throttle setting. Below the optimum altitude the Mach number for long range cruise decreases with increasing altitude.

5.6   Step climbs

A cruise climb is usually not compatible with Air Traffic Control requirements. A profile approximating to a cruise climb, called a step climb, is therefore flown instead. The aeroplane is climbed to the first semicircular cruising level approximately 1000' above optimum altitude and cruises level at the optimum Mach number until it is approximately 3000' below optimum altitude, at which point it is climbed 4000' to the next semicircular cruising level.

Step climbs are used on long distance flights to fly as close as possible to the optimum altitude as aeroplane mass decreases

V_{MRC} is anyway not a practical speed because of speed instability. A 1%, reduction in SAR is therefore adopted to overcome this problem and the resulting long range cruise speed, V_{LRC}, nets a noticeable speed advantage over V_{MRC}. For practical reasons, V_{LRC} is generally calculated as V_{MRC} in a 100 KT headwind. V_{LRC} varies with mass and density altitude.

CRANFIELD AVIATION TRAINING SCHOOL LTD. PART-FCL ATO N° 276
CATS INNOVATION CENTRE, LUTON, Bedfordshire LU2 8DL U.K.   www.catsaviation.com

5-5

Performance

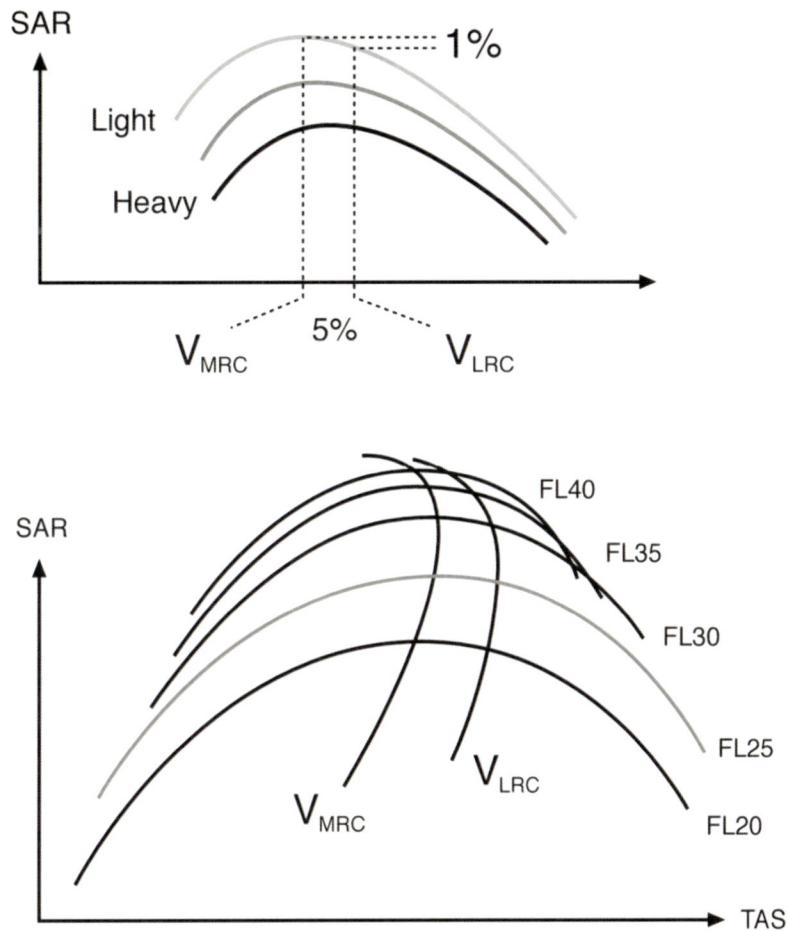

Figure 5.4 V$_{MRC}$ corresponds to the best SAR and varies with altitude. At V$_{LRC}$ a 1% loss of range is traded for a gain in speed of approximately 5% (top)

5.6.1   The effect of 1 or 2 engines inoperative on specific range

With one or two engines inoperative the best specific range at high altitude (assume altitude remains constant) is reduced.

5.6.2   The effect of mass on maximum range

The traffic load can be limited by the desired range.

5.6.3   The effect of CG position on maximum range

The centre of gravity positioned near but still within the aft limit improves the maximum range because there is less trim drag.

5.7   Optimum altitude

The optimum altitude increases as mass decreases and is the altitude at which the specific range reaches its maximum. In practice, an aeroplane sometimes flies above or below the optimum altitude because optimum altitude increases continuously during flight.

CRANFIELD AVIATION TRAINING SCHOOL LTD. PART-FCL ATO N° 276
CATS INNOVATION CENTRE, LUTON, Bedfordshire LU2 8DL U.K.

www.catsaviation.com

5-6

Performance

5.8   Absolute ceiling and Service ceiling

Since maximum climb rate for an aeroplane decreases with increasing altitude it follows that at a given altitude it will be zero. This corresponds to the altitude for which the power required and power available curves are tangential to each other. This altitude is called absolute ceiling. At this altitude only one speed is available.

> Absolute ceiling is the altitude at which the rate of climb theoretically is zero

Absolute ceiling is an impractical altitude to operate at because of speed instability, therefore another altitude referred to as service ceiling is specified. At the service ceiling there is a reasonable, though still narrow, range of speed within which the aeroplane can operate.

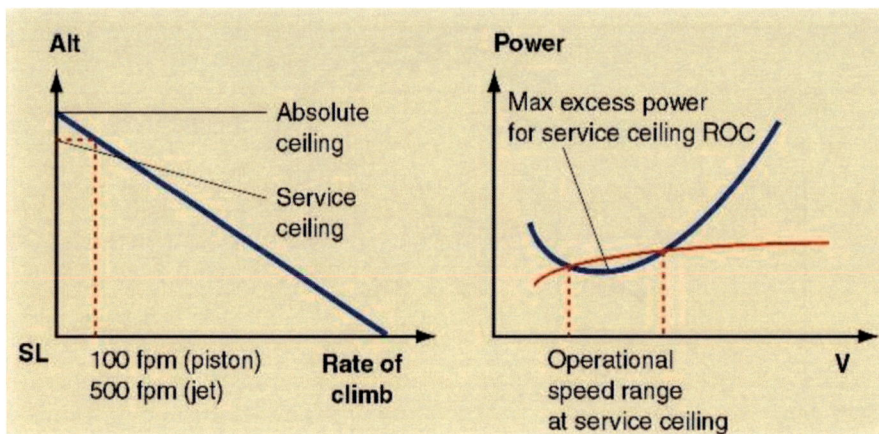

Figure 5.5 At absolute ceiling rate of climb is zero, however, at service ceiling excess power and the available speed range remain very limited

> A higher mass results in a lower rate of climb and hence lower absolute and service ceilings

5.9   Aerodynamic ceiling

For jet aeroplanes operating at high altitude, speed range is restricted not only by performance factors but also aerodynamically. This results in an aerodynamic ceiling being reached. Indicated stall speed (low speed stall) and associated buffet onset speed increase slowly with increasing altitude. Minimum speed is therefore higher at altitude. In contrast, at high altitudes, Mach effects make the boundary layer around parts of the aeroplane more turbulent. This is called high speed buffet (high speed stall) and results in control problems if the speed is increased further. Indicated airspeed for high speed buffet onset decreases with increasing altitude and weight.

> Because low speed buffet onset increases and high speed buffet decreases with increasing altitude, the available speed range becomes narrower. At a certain altitude and weight the limiting speeds coincide

In addition, with regard to the load factor imposed, a 40° bank turn in a 15 tonne aeroplane is equivalent to level flight in the same aeroplane with a gross mass of 19.5 tonnes. The associated 1.3G load factor is generally adopted as a manoeuvring safety factor when cruise flight level is selected, allowing a bank angle of 40° before stalling. The danger associated with low speed and / or high speed buffet limits the manoeuvring load factor at high altitude.

> Aerodynamic ceiling is the altitude at which the speeds for low speed buffet and high speed buffet are the same

5.10 Maximum operating altitude

The maximum operating altitude for an aeroplane with a pressurised cabin is the highest pressure altitude certified for normal operation.

5.11 Flight over high ground

If a twin engined aeroplane in cruise flight with one engine inoperative has to fly over high ground, in order to maintain the highest possible altitude the speed corresponding to the maximum value of the lift / drag ratio should be flown.

5.12 En route one and two engines inoperative and drift down

Drift down is a procedure to be applied after engine failure if the aeroplane is above the 1 engine out maximum altitude. JAR-OPS 1.500 and 1.505 require an Aeroplane in Performance Class A to be able to continue flight, with one engine having failed at the most critical point en route, or two engines simultaneously if the aeroplane has three or more engines, from cruising altitude to an aerodrome where a landing can be made, clearing all terrain and obstructions within 5 NM of track by at least 2000' vertically and such that the net flight path has a positive gradient at least 1000' above such obstructions and 1500' above the landing aerodrome.

En route	5 NM track clearance	Landing aerodrome
1000'	2000'	1500'

An operator must increase the width of the obstacle domain from within 5 NM to within 10 NM of track if required navigation performance does not meet a 95% containment level, that is, if it is unable to remain within the corridor for at least 95% of its flying time in that airspace. It is assumed that ice protection systems, reducing aeroplane performance, will be in use at the time of failure if icing conditions are forecast. Fuel jettisoning is permitted.

Number of engines	Diminishment in actual climb performance	
	1 engine inoperative	2 engines inoperative
2	- 1.1%	
3	- 1.4%	- 0.3%
4	- 1.6%	- 0.5%

Table 5.1 One and two engine inoperative net flight paths are derived from gross climb performance diminished by amounts specified in JAR 25.123(b) and (c). For aeroplanes in Performance Class B JAR-OPS 1.540 states that the gross gradient is increased by 0.5% to provide the assumed one engine inoperative en route gradient, allowing the aeroplane to fly to 1000' above an aerodrome at which performance requirements can be met, during which at no point must the aeroplane be assumed to be flying above an altitude at which rate of climb exceeds 300 fpm with all engines at maximum continuous power

The net drift down path is steeper and terminates at a lower stabilizing pressure altitude than the actual drift down path

The drift down path is not a constant angle of descent, but instead becomes shallower as descent progresses. The profile is constructed using the hypotenuses of altitude triangles, representing the gradient for the mid-height of altitude bands of interval 2000' or 4000', starting at cruising altitude and continuing down to stabilizing altitude.

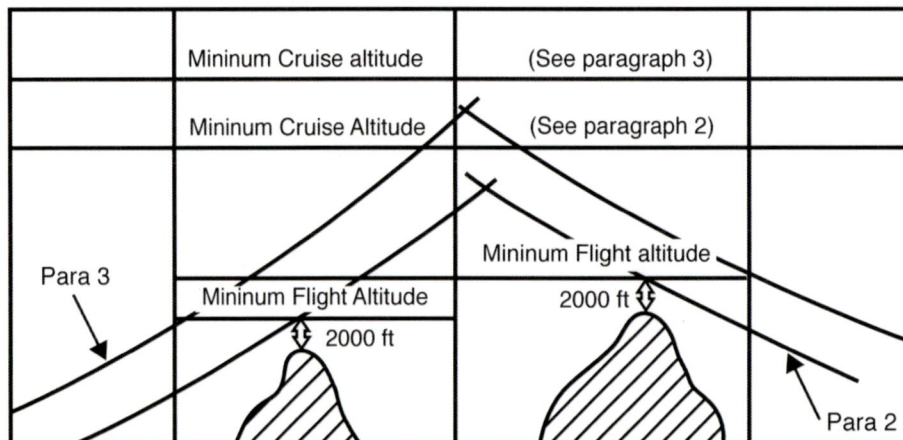

Figure 5.6 From AMC OPS 1.500

5.13 Re-light

Where a power unit fails above maximum relight altitude the usual procedure is to initiate a normal one engine inoperative descent to maximum relight altitude.

5.14 ETOPS

Regulations for extended range operation of two-engined aeroplanes, Extended Twin Operations (ETOPS), are addressed by JAR-OPS 1.246. These are divided into two parts, one part to be observed by the manufacturer during construction of an ETOPS aeroplane and the other by the operator. During manufacture, the powerplant, electrical and hydraulic systems must prove reliable for an extended time, in the latter cases with or without engine failure. JAR-OPS specifies that, unless approved for ETOPS, two-engined aeroplanes must not operate on a route further from an adequate aerodrome than, in the case of Performance Class A aeroplanes with either a maximum approved passenger seating configuration of 20 or more or a MTOM of 45360 kg or more, the distance flown in 60 min at the one-engine-inoperative cruise speed, and for Performance Class B aeroplanes the distance flown in 120 min at the one-engine-inoperative cruise speed or 300 NM, whichever is less. The speed for the calculation of the maximum distance to an adequate aerodrome, not exceeding V_{MO}, is based on TAS and determined for ISA in level flight at maximum continuous thrust on the remaining engine at:
- FL170 for turbojet aeroplanes
- FL80 for turboprop and piston engine aeroplanes or, if less:
- At the maximum flight level to which the aeroplane, with one engine inoperative, can climb, and maintain, using the gross rate of climb specified in the Aircraft Flight Manual and with a mass not less than that resulting from:
- MTOM at sea level
- All engine climb to the optimum long range cruise altitude
- All engines cruise at the long range cruise speed at this altitude until the time elapsed is equal to the thresholds specified.

The first level of extension attainable for an operator is an increase from 60 to 75 min range. An aeroplane approved for 120 min ETOPS must normally have shown at least 250000 engine hours and an in-flight shut-down ratio of 0.05 per 1000 h or less. To achieve a 120 min ETOPS approval, the operator must have completed at least 12 months of in-service operation with the aeroplane/engine configuration to be used, a requirement not necessary to get a 75 min approval. For further extension to 180 min ETOPS the aeroplane/engine combination must show in-flight shut-down ratios of 0.02 per 1000 engine hours or less. The operator must have accumulated an additional 12 months of documented operation with that configuration.

Self Assessment Test 05

1   What effect has a tailwind on the maximum endurance speed?
A)   The IAS will be increased
B)   The IAS will be decreased
C)   Tailwind only effects holding speed
D)   No effect

2   On a twin engined piston aircraft with variable pitch propellers, for a given mass and altitude, the minimum drag speed is 125 KT and the holding speed (minimum fuel burn per hour) is 90 KT. The best rate of climb speed will be obtained for a speed:
A)   Less than 90 KT
B)   equal to 90 KT
C)   is between 90 and 125 KT
D)   equal to 125 KT

3   Considering TAS for maximum range and maximum endurance, other factors remaining constant,
A)   TAS for maximum range will increase with increased altitude while TAS for maximum endurance will decrease with increased altitude
B)   both will stay constant regardless of altitude
C)   both will decrease with increasing altitude
D)   both will increase with increasing altitude

4   During climb with all engines, the altitude where the rate of climb reduces to 100 fpm is called:
A)   Service ceiling
B)   Maximum transfer ceiling
C)   Absolute ceiling
D)   Thrust ceiling

5   The absolute ceiling
A)   is the altitude at which the rate of climb theoretically is zero
B)   is the altitude at which the best climb gradient attainable is 5%
C)   is the altitude at which the aeroplane reaches a maximum rate of climb of 100 fpm
D)   can be reached only with minimum steady flight speed

6   The maximum rate of climb that can be maintained at the absolute ceiling is:
A)   0 fpm
B)   100 fpm
C)   125 fpm
D)   500 fpm

7   The pilot of a light twin engine aircraft has calculated a 4000 m service ceiling, based on the forecast general conditions for the flight and a take-off mass of 3250 kg. If the take-off mass is 3000 kg, the service ceiling will be:
A)   unchanged, equal to 4000 m
B)   less than 4000 m
C)   higher than 4000 m
D)   only a new performance analysis will determine if the service ceiling is higher or lower than 4000 m

CRANFIELD AVIATION TRAINING SCHOOL LTD. PART-FCL ATO N° 276
CATS INNOVATION CENTRE, LUTON, Bedfordshire LU2 8DL U.K.   www.catsaviation.com

CATS

5-10   Performance

8   For a piston engined aeroplane, the speed for maximum range is:
A)   that which gives the maximum lift to drag ratio
B)   that which gives the minimum value of drag
C)   that which gives the maximum value of lift
D)   1.4 times the stall speed in clean configuration

9   Maximum endurance for a piston engined aeroplane is achieved at:
A)   The speed that approximately corresponds to the maximum rate of climb speed
B)   The speed for maximum lift coefficient
C)   The speed for minimum drag
D)   The speed that corresponds to the speed for maximum climb angle

10   The speed for maximum lift/drag ratio will result in:
A)   The maximum angle of climb for a propeller driven aeroplane
B)   The maximum range for a jet aeroplane
C)   The maximum range for a propeller driven aeroplane
D)   The maximum endurance for a propeller driven aeroplane

Self Assessment Test 05 Answers

1	D
2	B
3	D
4	A
5	A
6	A
7	C
8	A
9	A
10	C

CRANFIELD AVIATION TRAINING SCHOOL LTD. PART-FCL ATO N° 276
CATS INNOVATION CENTRE, LUTON, Bedfordshire LU2 8DL U.K.

www.catsaviation.com

5-12

Performance

CHAPTER 6
Descent and Approach

6.1 Resolving vectors

The forces acting on the gliding aeroplane are lift, drag and weight, these being in equilibrium.

Lift is related to weight such that

$$\text{lift} \;=\; \text{weight} \;\times\; \cos\theta$$

Drag is related to weight such that

$$\text{drag} \;=\; \text{weight} \;\times\; \sin\theta$$

Since cotangent (cot) is the result of cosine divided by sine

$$\cot\theta \;=\; \frac{\text{lift}}{\text{drag}}$$

> The angle of glide θ is determined solely by the lift to drag ratio, thus the best gliding angle is independent of weight
>
> Weight only influences forward speed down the glideslope

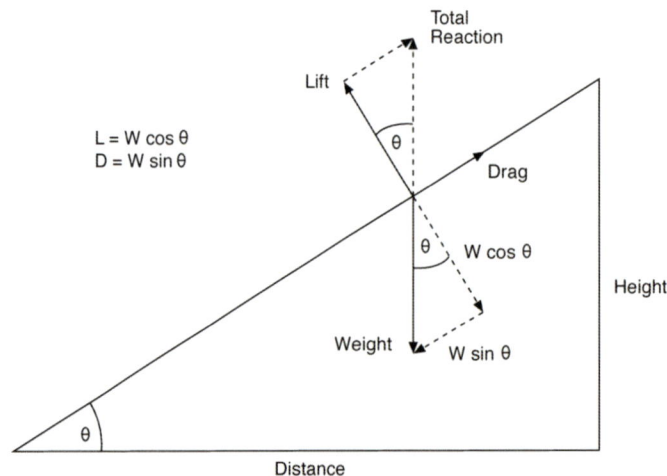

Figure 6.1 Forces acting on an aeroplane in a glide descent are lift, normal to the flight path and drag, parallel to the flight path, and weight vertically downwards

> In steady descending flight the forces acting on the aeroplane are:
>
> $$T + W \sin\gamma = D$$
>
> (T = Thrust, W = Weight, γ descent angle, D = Drag)

CRANFIELD AVIATION TRAINING SCHOOL LTD. PART-FCL ATO N° 276
CATS INNOVATION CENTRE, LUTON, Bedfordshire LU2 8DL U.K.   www.catsaviation.com

6-1   Performance

6.2 Minimum rate of descent and glide angle

The rate of climb depends on the difference between the power available and the power required. As the power available is reduced beyond the point where power available equals power required the aeroplane will only descend. The aeroplane will descend with the minimum rate of descent at the speed where the power required is minimum. At this point the distance between the power required curve and the *x*-axis is the shortest.

6.3 Gliding

Gliding implies a steady descent at constant IAS with no power. There is therefore no thrust vector. Potential energy derived from weight may be split into two vectors: one to balance lift and the other to balance drag.

Forward vector = weight x sin descent angle
Downward vector = weight x cosine descent angle.

Gliding for endurance (as long as possible in terms of time) means that the aircraft must descend at the lowest rate. A greater mass will increase the rate of descent. A greater mass decreases gliding endurance. Wind does not affect gliding endurance.

The minimum glide angle occurs where the ratio between the power required and the speed is minimum. On the power versus airspeed graph, the best ratio between the two parameters occurs at the tangent to the curve of a straight line from the origin. Recall that the speed with the best power required to speed ratio is also that speed for minimum drag. Thus the speed for minimum glide angle is also that speed for best ratio of lift to drag.

Angle of descent in a glide is affected by configuration and angle of attack

6.3.1 The effect of mass on gliding performance

Increased mass increases the speed for the best angle of descent of a gliding aeroplane.

If an aeroplane executes a steady glide at the speed for minimum glide angle with the forward speed kept constant the effect of a lower mass is to increase the rate of descent, increase the glide angle and decrease the CL/CD ratio.

With less mass there is less lift-induced drag and V_{MD} decreases. To maintain the same forward speed the nose is pitched down further which increases the glide angle. A decreased angle of attack decreases the coefficient of lift, which has the effect of decreasing the CL/CD ratio.

A decreased mass increases the gliding endurance.

CRANFIELD AVIATION TRAINING SCHOOL LTD. PART-FCL ATO N° 276
CATS INNOVATION CENTRE, LUTON, Bedfordshire LU2 8DL U.K.   www.catsaviation.com

6-2

Performance

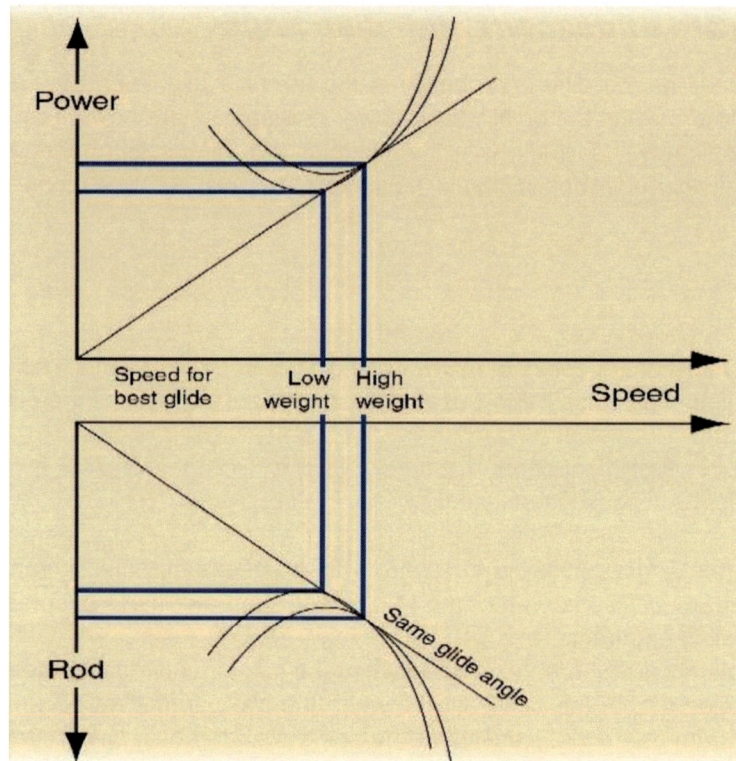

Figure 6.2 As weight increases, so does the rate of descent and minimum drag speed, due to the shifting downwards and to the right of the curve

6.4 Effect of wind on descent performance

The wind does not affect the speed for the minimum rate of descent since rate of descent is independent of the speed relative to the ground. The glide angle, conversely, is greatly affected by the wind, because the wind affects the ground speed. In a headwind, the glideslope is steeper and the airspeed higher. The converse is true for a tailwind.

A constant headwind increases the angle of the descent flight path

6.5 Piston-propeller aeroplane descent

For piston-propeller aeroplanes a glide descent is not practical, because at idle power the propeller produces significant drag. The gliding angle is therefore rather steep, and the resulting glide ratio for a typical light aeroplane descending at idle power is about 8:1. In addition, reciprocating engines are very susceptible to air cooling at idle power.

For the comfort of the passengers, because the ambient pressure increases during descent, rate of descent is kept as low as possible. 500 feet per minute is appropriate for an unpressurized aeroplane.

6.6 Jet aeroplane descent

Jet engines do not produce much drag at idle power. Jet aeroplanes therefore have a comparably high glide ratio - a Boeing 747 has a glide ratio of 18:1 when flown at the speed for best glide. Descending at this speed gives a fuel optimum descent. The speed for best glide is however often too low to be used as the operational descent speed because of speed instability and a small margin to the stall. A slightly higher speed that offers speed stability and better stall margins may therefore be used, called optimum descent speed. A still higher normal descent speed is often preferred to save time. The normal descent speed is usually constant and independent of the aeroplane mass. As a result, the normal descent speed is closer to the optimum descent speed for greater aeroplane mass, thus the descent gradient is better for a heavy aeroplane than for a light aeroplane. The descent may be flown at the maximum speed limiting values M_{MO} and V_{MO}. The higher speed during the descent increases the drag, and this descent will therefore be steeper, allowing for a later top of descent. As with unpressurized aeroplanes, the rate of descent must be limited for the sake of passenger comfort. In icing conditions, a certain amount of thrust must be maintained in order to allow for anti-ice bleed air. The descent rate will be lower than in a normal descent. Most aeroplanes need a certain amount of thrust to maintain cabin pressure during initial descent from upper altitudes. A common procedure is to start the descent with a lower rate of descent, without reducing thrust to idle. As an altitude where the pressurizing system can perform with the engine idling is approached the thrust is reduced to idle and the normal descent profile is re-established. When encountering turbulence en route, the speed is reduced by reducing thrust. In the descent, thrust is already zero and speed must be reduced by using speedbrakes or other drag-producing devices. Speedbrakes are usually certified for use up to V_{MO} / M_{MO}. Following a rapid decompression it is essential to descend to 10000' or lower as quickly as possible. Emergency descent is performed with idle thrust, speedbrakes deployed and speed increased to V_{MO} / M_{MO}. The resulting descent rates are generally around 9000 fpm.

6.7   The approach

During the approach phase the aeroplane configuration is gradually changed from clean to the landing configuration. The speed is reduced from the descent speed to threshold speed. The descent is generally finished some distance before the approach phase commences to allow for a speed reduction in level flight to a maximum initial approach speed.

6.7.1 Landing gear speeds

The speed V_{LO} is defined as landing gear operating speed. The speed V_{LE} is defined as the maximum speed at which the aeroplane may be safely flown with the landing gear extended. V_{LO} is usually a speed lower than V_{LE}.

6.7.2 Approach speeds

Minimum approach speeds are related to the stall speed so that normal turns can be made during the initial approach. These minimum speeds are 1.4 to 1.5 times V_{S1}. As more high lift devices are selected during the approach the associated stall speed decreases and so does the approach speed.

During the final approach, because the bank angles are smaller, the minimum speeds can be further reduced, typically down to 1.3 V_{S1} plus five knots.

> The approach phase ends over the runway threshold with the speed 1.3 times V_{S0}

LANDING			32 t	LANDING			42 t
FL	*<250*	*250- 290*	*>290*	*FL*	*<250*	*250- 290*	*>290*
V_{HOLD}	183	193	203	V_{HOLD}	208	218	228
	Clean ..183	GO-AROUND			Clean ..208	GO-AROUND	
	0.........151	V2 5.........151			0.........172	V2 5.........139	
V_P	5.........140	VFl UP.......140		V_P	5.........160	VFl UP.......145	
	15.......128	Vsl IN.......128			15.......147	Vsl IN........170	
	25.......124	VClean.......124			25........169	VClean.......192	
V_A	25.......118			V_A	25........134		
FLAPS	50°	40°	25°	*FLAPS*	50°	40°	25°
V_A	113	117	118	V_A	128	133	134
V_{TH}	108	112	116	V_{TH}	123	128	133

Figure 6.3 Unlike light aeroplanes, heavy aeroplanes having larger flaps and slats have a wide range of stall speeds, hence approach speeds vary greatly with different flap settings. The mass range of large aeroplanes is also wide and therefore significant when selecting approach speeds

6.7.3 Jet engine spool up time and speed brakes

Propeller aeroplanes, especially piston-propeller aeroplanes, respond quickly when power is applied. In case of a go-around, high power can quickly be attained, thus low power and associated small flap settings can be used until the last part of the final approach where speed is reduced to threshold speed. Jet engines have a long spool up time from low to high thrust. To prepare for a possible go-around more flap is deployed earlier in the final approach to maintain a certain thrust setting and thus reduce the spool up time if a go-around has to be initiated. Go-around thrust is a certified rating.

Speed control during the approach is performed by balancing thrust and drag. The speed of propeller aeroplanes is easily controlled with the throttle, the propeller immediately producing thrust when power is applied. Due to their long spool up time jet engines respond sluggishly on advancement of the throttle levers and do not produce significant drag when thrust is decreased.

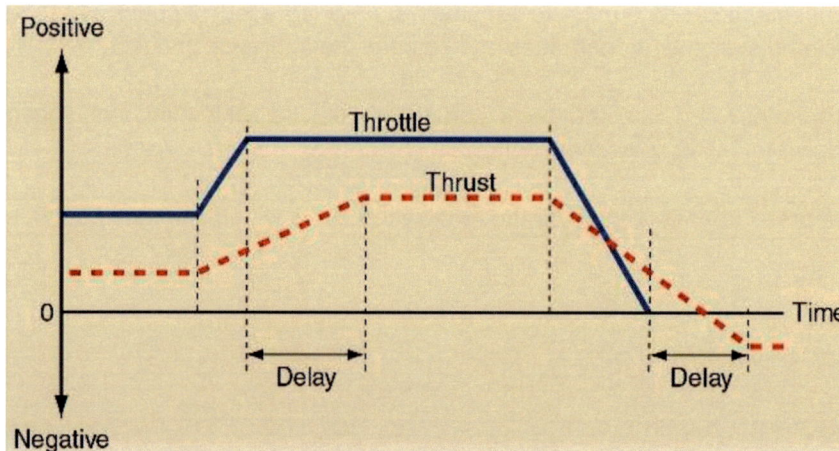

Figure 6.4 Due to their long spool up time jet engines respond sluggishly on advancement of the throttle levers and do not produce significant drag when thrust is decreased. Drag producing devices such as speed brakes may be required

6.7.4 Wind

Wind affects the approach considerably since the aeroplane is flown at speeds relative to the air at the same time as it must follow a pattern relative to the ground

In a headwind the aeroplane travels with a groundspeed that is lower than the airspeed. As the aeroplane follows a fixed glideslope the rate of descent is lower than on the same glideslope in zero wind. Because of the lower rate of descent, more power is required to maintain the correct approach speed. The converse is true during a tailwind approach.

6.8 Landing

Landing distance available (LDA) is that declared by an aerodrome authority as available for landing. LDA must be free of all non-frangible obstacles and have uniform slope, bearing strength and braking coefficient. It commences at runway threshold and extends for the length of the runway. The threshold may be displaced to allow for obstacles in the approach path, so foreshortening LDA.

Landing distance is that necessary to come to a complete stop from screen height in the landing configuration

Increased mass means higher kinetic energy, $\frac{1}{2}mv^2$, higher stall speed and consequently higher threshold speed and a greater landing distance.

Mass is the only parameter that may be adjusted to reduce the landing distance

At low temperatures and altitudes TAS is close to, or even lower than, IAS. The threshold speed is low and the landing distance shorter. The converse is true for high temperatures and altitudes.

6.9 Factors affecting Landing

	Landing distance	Go-around performance
Increased altitude	↑	↓
Increased temperature	↑	↓
Increased pressure	↓	↑
Increased mass	↑	↓
Upslope	↓	
Headwind	↓	
Flap	↓	↓
A/C packs off	↓	
Engine anti-ice on	↑	
Antiskid inoperative	↑	

Table 6.1 Factors affecting landing (A/C: Air-Conditioning)

CRANFIELD AVIATION TRAINING SCHOOL LTD. PART-FCL ATO N° 276
CATS INNOVATION CENTRE, LUTON, Bedfordshire LU2 8DL U.K.   www.catsaviation.com

6-6

Performance

For Aeroplanes in Performance Class A JAR-OPS 1.515 and 1.520 state that

on a dry runway, turbojet aeroplanes must be able to stop within 60% of LDA and turboprop within 70% LDA, introducing safety factors for LDA of 1.67 and 1.43 times the landing distance respectively

if the landing runway is forecast to be wet LDA must be at least 1.15 times the landing distance

the factored landing distance required (LDR) includes correction for not more than 50% of headwind and not less than 150% of tailwind and for runway slope if it exceeds ± 2%

Example:

For a turboprop powered aeroplane, a 2000 m long runway at the destination aerodrome is forecast to be wet. The dry runway landing distance, should not exceed:

2000 m / 1.43 = 1398.6 m

1398.6 m / 1.15 = 1216.2 m

According to JAR-OPS 1.550 and 1.555 the landing requirements for aeroplanes in Performance Class B are the same as those for turboprop aeroplanes in Performance Class A, accounting also for a safety factor of 1.15 for grass runways and with the exception of contaminated runways, on which for Performance Class B the landing distance need only be less than or equal to LDA.

6.10 Missed approach and baulked landing

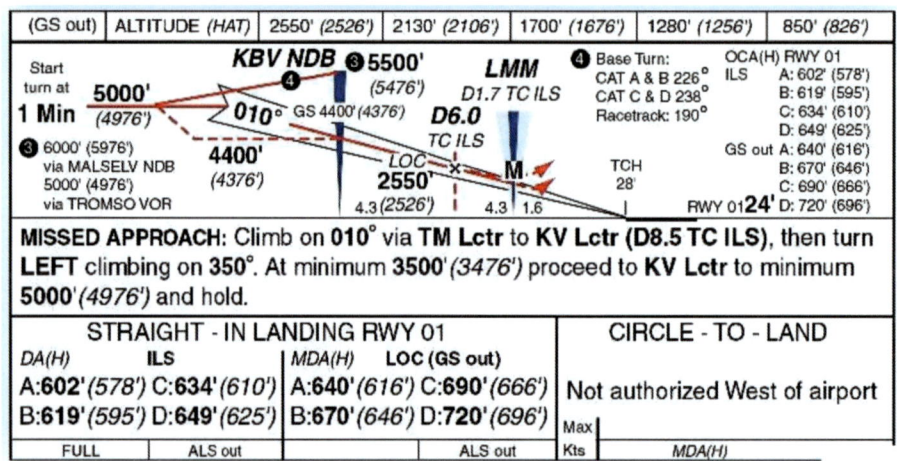

Figure 6.2 In the case of a missed approach obstacle clearance and manoeuvring capability are considered through the approach climb and landing climb requirements. Performance requirements do not account for obstacle clearance following a missed approach - this requirement is accounted for by the missed approach procedure

According to JAR 25.121(d) the approach climb requirement is based on

- Critical engine inoperative, remaining engines at go-around thrust
- Gear up
- Approach flap

At maximum landing weight for the prevailing conditions, at a discontinued approach speed not exceeding 1.5 V_S and with a minimum gross climb gradient of not less than 2.1%, 2.4% and 2.7% for two, three and four-engine aeroplanes respectively, the approach climb requirements are satisfied. The requirements may limit the flap setting used during an approach with one engine inoperative. In an emergency, fuel jettisoning may be used to achieve the requirements.

If, however, an instrument approach is made with a decision height below 200 feet JAR-OPS 1.510(b) states that the aeroplane must be able to execute a missed approach with the critical engine failed having a gradient of at least 2.5%, or the published gradient, whichever is higher.

Beyond decision height an aeroplane is committed to landing unless, in the event of the runway becoming blocked during the landing run and with all engines operating, a baulked landing is executed. The climb made following a baulked landing is called a landing climb.

According to JAR 25.119 the landing climb requirement is based on
- All engines at go-around thrust
- Gear down
- Landing flap

The aeroplane is climbed at a landing climb speed of 1.15 V_S for four-engined aeroplanes and 1.2 V_S for all other aeroplanes and with a minimum gross climb gradient of 3.2%.

Similar requirements for aeroplanes in Performance Class B are dictated by Appendix 1 to JAR-OPS 1.525(b):

With:
- Critical engine inoperative, remaining engines at not more than maximum continuous power
- Gear up
- Flaps up

the steady gradient of climb must be at least 0.75% at a climb speed not less than 1.2 V_{S1} at 1500'

With:
- All engines operating at not more than the power or thrust available 8 s after initiating movement of the power controls from minimum flight idle
- Gear down
- Landing flap

the steady gradient of climb must be at least 2.5% at a climb speed equal to V_{REF}.

Self Assessment Test 06

1 The lift coefficient (C_L) of a wing at a given angle of attack:
A) Is dependent on the surface area of the wing
B) Is increased by the use of high lift devices
C) Is constant and not affected by high lift devices
D) Is reduced when high lift devices are used

2 C_{LMAX} may be increased by the use of:
A) Flaps
B) Slats
C) Boundary layer control
D) All of the above

3 What is the effect on V_{MD} and speed stability of retracting an airbrake?
A) V_{MD} increases, speed stability remains unchanged
B) V_{MD} decreases, speed stability remains unchanged
C) V_{MD} increases, speed stability decreases
D) Both are increased

4 What is the effect on C_{LMAX} and the angle of attack when a trailing edge flap is retracted?
A) Critical angle decreases, C_{LMAX} decreases
B) Critical angle increases, C_{LMAX} decreases
C) Critical angle decreases, C_{LMAX} increases
D) Critical angle increases, C_{LMAX} increases

5 The greatest gliding range would be obtained from a wing at:
A) A high angle of attack at maximum lift/drag ratio
B) A small angle of attack at maximum lift/drag ratio
C) A small angle of attack at minimum lift/drag ratio
D) A high angle of attack at minimum lift/drag ratio

6 If an aircraft maintains a constant IAS, how does power required to overcome drag vary with altitude?
A) More power is required as altitude decreases
B) Power required increases with an increase in altitude
C) It is unaffected since drag is the same at a constant IAS
D) It is dependent on throttle setting

7 How is stalling speed affected by an increase in thrust from a jet engine, assuming that the aircraft is attempting to maintain straight and level flight?
A) There is an increase in stalling speed due to slipstream over the wing
B) There is a decrease in stalling speed due to slipstream over the wing
C) There is no change because there is no slipstream over the wing in a jet aircraft
D) An increase in thrust decreases stalling speed

8 What is absolute ceiling for a jet aircraft?
A) The altitude at which the rate of climb is 500 fpm
B) The altitude at which excess power is zero
C) The altitude at which the rate of climb is 100 fpm
D) The altitude at which the rate of climb is 150 fpm

CRANFIELD AVIATION TRAINING SCHOOL LTD. PART-FCL ATO N° 276
CATS INNOVATION CENTRE, LUTON, Bedfordshire LU2 8DL U.K.

www.catsaviation.com

6-9

Performance

9   Assuming that an aircraft is maintaining straight and level flight at V$_{MD}$ approximately, what would be the angle of attack?
A)   10°
B)   17°
C)   4°
D)   0°

10   Gliding angle is:
A)   Directly proportional to L:D ratio
B)   Inversely proportional to L:D ratio
C)   Directly proportional to weight
D)   Inversely proportional to weight

11   At a given mass, the stalling speed of a twin engine aircraft is 100 kt in the landing configuration. The minimum speed a pilot must maintain in short final is:
A)   115 KT
B)   120 KT
C)   130 KT
D)   125 KT

12   A runway is contaminated with 0.5 cm of wet snow. The flight manual of a light twin nevertheless authorises a landing in these conditions. The landing distance will be, in relation to that for a dry runway:
A)   increased
B)   reduced
C)   substantially decreased
D)   unchanged

13   What is the effect of increased mass on the performance of a gliding aeroplane?
A)   There is no effect
B)   The speed for best angle of descent increases
C)   The lift/drag ratio decreases
D)   The gliding angle decreases

14   An aircraft has two certified landing flaps positions, 25° and 35°. If a pilot chooses 25° instead of 35°, the aircraft will have:
A)   a reduced landing distance and degraded go-around performance
B)   a reduced landing distance and better go-around performance
C)   an increased landing distance and better go-around performance
D)   an increased landing distance and degraded go-around performance

15   An aeroplane is in a power off glide at best gliding speed. If the pilot increases pitch attitude the glide distance:
A)   decreases
B)   may increase or decrease depending on the aeroplane
C)   increases
D)   remains the same

16 Two identical aeroplanes at different masses are descending at idle thrust. Which of the following statements correctly describes their descent characteristics?
A) At a given angle of attack the lighter aeroplane will always glide further than the heavier aeroplane
B) At a given angle of attack, both the vertical and the forward speed are greater for the heavier aeroplane
C) At a given angle of attack the heavier aeroplane will always glide further than the lighter aeroplane
D) There is no difference between the descent characteristics of the two aeroplanes

17 Which of the following factors will lead to an increase of ground distance during a glide, while maintaining the appropriate minimum glide angle speed?
A) Tailwind
B) Headwind
C) Increase of aircraft mass
D) Decrease of aircraft mass

Self Assessment Test 06 Answers

1	B
2	D
3	C
4	B
5	A
6	B
7	C
8	B
9	C
10	B
11	C
12	A
13	B
14	C
15	A
16	B
17	A

CRANFIELD AVIATION TRAINING SCHOOL LTD. PART-FCL ATO N° 276
CATS INNOVATION CENTRE, LUTON, Bedfordshire LU2 8DL U.K.

www.catsaviation.com

6-12

Performance

CHAPTER 7

V speeds

Approach-Climb Speed This is the recommended speed for initial climb-out after a missed approach is initiated at or above decision height. It ensures that the aircraft, with the critical power-unit inoperative, at the maximum landing weight and in the configuration achieved 15 s after initiation (i.e. undercarriage retracted), will be able to maintain the minimum climb gradient required. For Class A aeroplanes the gradient is 2.1% for twin-engined aircraft, 2.4% for three-engined aircraft and 2.7% for four-engined aircraft. The speed must not exceed 1.5Vs. *JAR* 25.121 *(d)* (3).

Buffet Speed This is the speed at which the aerodynamic airflow becomes turbulent and causes uncontrollable vibration of the airframe. *JAR* 25.251.

Calibrated Airspeed (CAS) is the indicated airspeed, corrected for position and instrument error. It is equal to True Airspeed at MSL in a Standard Atmosphere. *JAR* 1 *page* 1-3 *and ICAO Annex* 6 *page* 44.

Cruising Speed The representative TAS, quoted to the nearest 10 KT, used for aeroplanes of the type to calculate their compliance with AN(G)Rs regarding over-water flight and two-engines-inoperative data.

Equivalent Airspeed (EAS) The Calibrated Airspeed corrected for compressibility at the particular pressure altitude under consideration. It is equal to Calibrated Airspeed in a Standard Atmosphere. *JAR* 1 *page* 1-6.

Flaps-Up Safety Speed (FUSS) (V2 0^0 Flap). This speed is the safety speed used during the fourth segment of a six-segment net flight path for older turbo-propeller aeroplanes. It is equal to 1.2Vs. Sometimes it is called the Initial En-Route Climb Speed.

Indicated Airspeed (IAS) is the speed as shown by the pitot / static airspeed indicator calibrated to reflect Standard Atmosphere adiabatic compressible flow at MSL and uncorrected for airspeed system errors. *JAR* 1 *page* 1-8.

Landing Approach Speed The calibrated airspeed in the landing configuration that must be maintained down to screen height 50' during a stabilized approach. It must not be less than 1.3Vs at any practicable landing weight. *JAR* 25.125(a).

Landing-Climb Speed This is the recommended speed for the initial climb-out after a baulked landing. It ensures that the aircraft, with *all-power-units-operating* and in the landing configuration, at the power obtained eight seconds after initiation, achieves a minimum gross gradient of climb of 3.2%. The speed, which is never less than VMCL and must not exceed the greater of 1.3Vs and VMCL, is exactly determined by AUW and the flap-setting on landing. It is 1.15Vs for four-engined aeroplanes and 1.2Vs for all other Class A aeroplanes. *JAR* 25.119(b).

Maximum Abandonment Speed The highest speed from which a take-off with all engines operating on a very slippery or contaminated surface can be abandoned with a reasonable degree of safety. It does not guarantee the aeroplane will stop within the Accelerate/Stop Distance Available. It is *not* a V1 speed, and does not imply an ability to continue take-off after suffering an engine failure. It may well be lower than VMCG.

Normal One-Engine-Inoperative Cruise Speed The TAS calculated, for ISA conditions from the one-engine-inoperative cruise control data for the aeroplane, at the AUW obtained two hours after take-off at the

CRANFIELD AVIATION TRAINING SCHOOL LTD. PART-FCL ATO N° 276
CATS INNOVATION CENTRE, LUTON, Bedfordshire LU2 8DL U.K.

CATS

www.catsaviation.com

7-1

Performance

maximum authorized TOW and climbing to and maintaining the all-engines-operating optimum initial cruise level for long range cruise.

True Airspeed (TAS) True Airspeed is the Equivalent Airspeed corrected for density error and is the true speed of the aircraft relative to the undisturbed air. *JAR 1 page 1-12.*

V1 Commonly referred to as decision speed, V1 is determined by the relative field- lengths, aircraft configuration and AUW and is the speed at which the pilot, in the event of a power unit failure, must decide whether to abandon or to continue the take-off. It is at this speed that the aircraft can be safely brought to rest on the ground or safely become airborne. Engine failure before this speed demands the abandonment of take-off. Above this speed the aircraft is committed to becoming airborne even if an engine fails.
If TOW is less than the maximum TOW determined by the field-lengths, a range of V1 is available. Turbo-jet aircraft generally use the lower value, dictated by the actual TOW. Piston or turbo-prop aircraft should use the higher value, determined by the field lengths. The manufacturer may alternatively recommend a value to use. V1 is never less than VEF plus the speed increase after engine failure to the point at which the pilot applies the first means of retardation, nor greater than VR or VMBE. There is a two-second delay built into V1 to allow for the recognition of and the reaction to the failure by the pilot. *JAR 25. 107(a)(2).*

V1/VR ratio The power-failure speed ratio is one of the parameters used in the Flight Manual as a convenient method of presenting take-off data. The V1/V2 ratio was once used for this purpose, but has been superseded in modem Flight Manuals by the V1/VR ratio. Both VR and V2 are dependent on the aircraft AUW and flap setting. V1 is a variable determined by field-length and, aerodrome take-off conditions. If the AUW and V1/VR ratio are known, the calculation of V1 is a relatively simple procedure.

V2 The take-off safety speed, sometimes called the Free Air Safety Speed, is the speed which the aircraft is legally required to attain on reaching screen height with one-power-unit-inoperative. It varies with air density, TOW and flap setting, but must not be less than V2min or VR + the increment attained [according to JAR 25.111(c)(2)] before reaching screen height with the operative power units set at Maximum Take-off Power. *JAR 25.107(c) JAR 1 page 1-11.*

V2min The minimum take-off safety speed, is the minimum speed that V2 may be in terms of calibrated airspeed. It is never less than:

(1) 1.2Vs for
(a) Two-engined and three-engined turbo-prop aeroplanes; and
(b) Turbo-jet aeroplanes without provisions for obtaining a significant reduction in the one-engine-inoperative power-on stalling speed;
(2) 1.15Vs for
(a) Turbo-prop aeroplanes with more than three engines; and
(b) Turbo-jet aircraft with provisions for obtaining a significant reduction in the one-engine-inoperative power-on stalling speed; and
(3) 1.1 VMC. *JAR 25.107(b),. JAR 1 page 1-16.*

V3 The steady initial climb speed, with all-engines-operating, which must be achieved by screen height, and which is never less than V2 + 10 KT. *JAR 1 page 1-16.*

V4 The steady take-off climb speed, with all-engines-operating, using the scheduled techniques and achieved by 400' gross height. It is never less than 1.2 VMCA or 1.3VMS1, and is such that the gross flight path attained does not fall below the gross flight path from which the net flight path is derived.

V5 There is no official recognition or definition of this term, which is often incorrectly used to refer to the One-Engine-Inoperative En-route Climb Speed.

VA The design manoeuvring speed. *JAR 25.335(c).*

VAT -Target Threshold Speed -is the speed at which the pilot aims to cross the threshold when landing. It is an average speed calculated for *the conditions of light winds and slight turbulence,* and is determined by the AUW and flap setting. It may be related either to the all-power-units-operating condition (VAT_0), to the one-power-unit-inoperative (VAT_1 condition, or to the two-power-units-inoperative (VAT_2) condition. These terms were deleted from JAR 1 but are still used in JAR OPS 1.430(c) to categorize aeroplanes.

VATo That target threshold speed for an all-power-units-operating approach which is not less than any of the following:

(1) VMS1, + 22 KT, or *1.3VMSo*
(2) VMCL
(3) The minimum demonstrated threshold speed + 5 KT
(4) The final steady approach speed -10 KT
(5) 1.08 x the pre-stall buffet speed in steady flight

VAT_1 The target threshold speed for a one-power-unit-inoperative approach which is not less than any of the following:

(1) *VATo*
(2) VMCL (with the critical power unit inoperative) + 5 KT
(3) VMCL (with two power units inoperative) for three- and four-engined aircraft
(4) The final steady approach speed with the critical power unit inoperative - 10 KT

VB The design speed for maximum gust intensity. *JAR 25. 335 (d)*

VC The design cruising speed. *JAR 25. 335 (a)*

VD The design diving speed. *JAR 25.335(b)*

VDD The design drag devices speed. *JAR 25.335(f)*

VEF The calibrated speed at which, for the purposes of performance calculations, it is assumed that the most critical power unit fails. It is never less than VMCG. *JAR 25. 107(a)(1).*

VF The design flap speed. It may not be less than:

(1) $1.6VS_1$ with take-off flap at the maximum TOW.
(2) $1.8VS_1$ with approach flap at the maximum landing weight.
(3) $1.8VS_0$ with land flap at the maximum landing weight. *JAR 25.335(e)(3).*

VFE The maximum speed at which it is safe to fly with the flaps in a prescribed extended position. *JAR 25.1511,. JAR 1 pages* 1-7 & 1-15.

VFTO Final Take-Off Speed - the speed of the aeroplane at the end of the take-off path in the fourth segment, of a four segment net flight path, with *one power unit inoperative,* and the remaining engines set at the maximum continuous power setting, in the en-route configuration. The speed may not be less than 1.25Vs and the climb gradient may not be less than 1.2% for twin-engined aeroplanes, 1.5% for three-engined aircraft and 1.7% for four-engined aeroplanes. This speed is sometimes called the Final Segment Speed or the Final En-Route Climb Speed. *JAR 25.121(c) & JAR 1 pages* 1-6 & 1-15.

VGO This is the lowest decision speed from which a continued take-off is possible within the Take-Off Distance Available (TODA). *AMJ 25X1591 Paragraph 3.2.1.c Note.*

VIMD The velocity of minimum drag is the speed achieved at the lowest point of the total drag curve.

VIMP The velocity of minimum power is the speed attained at the lowest point on the power curve.

VLE The maximum speed at which the aeroplane may be safely flown with the undercarriage extended. *JAR 1 pages* 1-8 & 1-15 & *JAR 25.1515(b)*.

VLO The maximum speed at. which the undercarriage (landing gear) may be safely extended or retracted. *JAR 1 pages* 1-8 & 1-15, & *JAR 25.1515(a)*.

VLOF Lift-Off Speed - the speed at which the main wheels will leave the ground if the aircraft is rotated about its lateral axis at VR. It is a direct function of aircraft weight and flap setting, and is sometimes called Unstick Speed. *JAR 25.107(f)* & *JAR 1 page* 1-15.

VMBE Maximum Brake-Energy Speed - the maximum speed on the ground from which the aircraft can be safely brought to a halt within the energy-absorbing capabilities of the brakes. It may limit V1 in combinations of high TOW, temperature, altitude, downhill slope and tailwind.

VMC The Minimum Control Speed - the lowest calibrated airspeed at maximum take-off power at which, if the critical power unit suddenly becomes inoperative, it is possible to recover control to maintain a heading within *20°* of the original heading, without using more than 5° of bank. VMC is always greater than VMCG but may not exceed 1.2Vs. *JAR 25.149(b), (c)* & *(d) and ICAO Annex 6 page* 49.

VMCA The minimum control speed in the take-off climb. *JAR 1 page* 1-15.

VMCG The minimum control speed on the ground at maximum take-off power is such that, if the critical power unit becomes inoperative, it is possible *by aerodynamic means alone,* without the use of nosewheel steering, using normal piloting skill to maintain a parallel path not more than 30' laterally from the original path. VMCG is never greater than VMC. *JAR 25.149(e)*.

VMCL The minimum control speed on approach to land with *all engines operating* is the lowest speed that may be used for this phase of flight. It is obtainable at all power settings up to the maximum for level flight. It is such that, if a wing-mounted power unit becomes inoperative, it is possible to recover control using no more than 5° of bank so as to maintain straight flight without encountering flight characteristics which would prejudice maintenance of an accurate approach. *JAR* 25.149(f) & *JAR 1 page* 1-15.

VMCL₁ The minimum control speed on approach to land with *one-engine-inoperative*. It is such that it is possible to maintain straight flight using no more than 5° of bank without encountering flight characteristics which would prejudice maintenance of an accurate approach. *JAR 25.149(g)*.

VMCL₂ The minimum control speed on approach to land for three-engined and four-engined aeroplanes with *two-engines-inoperative*. It is such that it is possible to maintain straight flight using no more than 5° of bank without encountering flight characteristics which would prejudice maintenance of an accurate approach. *JAR 25. 149(h)*.

VMo / MMO The Maximum Operating Speed (or Mach number, whichever is critical at a particular altitude) which must not be deliberately exceeded in any flight condition. This speed is that which, allowing for moderate upsets, ensures the aircraft will remain free from buffet or other undesirable flying qualities associated with compressibility. It must not exceed VC. *JAR 25.1505*.

VMS The lowest possible stalling speed, Vs, for any combination of AUW and atmospheric conditions with power off, at which a large, not immediately controllable, pitching or rolling motion is encountered.

VMSo The lowest possible stalling speed, VSo (or if no stall is obtainable, the minimum steady-flight speed) with the wing-flaps in the landing setting, for any combination of AUW and atmospheric conditions.

VMS1 The lowest possible stalling speed, Vs₁ (or if no stall is obtainable, the minimum steady-flight speed) with the aeroplane in the configuration appropriate to the case under consideration, for any combination of AUW and atmospheric conditions.

VMU The lowest possible unstick speed, Vus, for any combination of AUW and atmospheric conditions, at and above which it is possible to leave the ground and climb, without undue hazard, to screen height, with all-power-units-operating. A margin of 5 KT between the lowest nose-wheel raising speed and VR would normally be considered adequate. *JAR 25.107(d), ACJ25.107(d).*

VNE The speed which must *never* be exceeded. *JAR* 1 *page* 1-15.

VP The Hydroplaning (Aquaplaning) Speed is the speed at which loss of directional control on the ground becomes total, by reason of the decrease in surface friction caused by contaminant on the runway surface.

VR Rotation Speed. This is the speed at which, in both the all-engines-operating and the one-engine-inoperative cases the makers recommend that on the take-off ground-run the pilot initiates a change in the aircraft attitude, by raising the nose- wheel and rotating the aircraft about its lateral axis, so that it lifts off the ground at a speed of not less than 1.1 VMu with all engines operating, or 1.05 VMu with one-engine-inoperative, and attains V2 on reaching screen height. VR is never less than V1 or 1.05 VMC. Its exact value depends on TOW and flap setting, and varies with pressure altitude and temperature. JAR 25.107(e), ACJ 25.107(e) & JAR 1 page 1-15.

VRA The speed recommended for the aeroplane to be flown in turbulence. It is not less than the maximum gust intensity speed, nor greater than (VMO - 35 KT). *JAR 25X1517; ACJ 25X1517 & JAR* 1 *page* 1-15.

VREF Reference Landing Speed - the speed of the aeroplane, in the specified landing configuration, at screen height, which is used to determine the landing distance for manual landings. *JAR* 1 *page* 1-11.

Vs The Calibrated Stalling Speed. It is not less than 94% of the minimum calibrated speed in flight at which the aeroplane can develop lift equal to its own weight for the configuration under consideration and is the minimum steady flight speed at which the aircraft remains controllable. *JAR 25.103(b) & JAR* 1 *page* 1-15.

VSo The stalling speed (or if no stalling speed is obtainable, the minimum steady-flight speed) with the wing-flaps in the landing setting. *JAR* 1 *page* 1-15 & *ICAO Annex* 6 *page* 45.

VS1 The stalling speed (or if no stalling speed is obtainable, the minimum steady-flight speed) with the aeroplane in the configuration appropriate to the case under consideration. *JAR* 1 *page* 1-15 & *ICAO Annex* 6 *page* 45.

VS1g The speed at which the aeroplane develops lift equal to its weight. It is Vs factorised to allow for the excess of weight over lift during the stall. *JAR 25.103(c) & JAR* 1 *page* 1-15.

VSR - The reference stalling speed.

VSRo -The reference stalling speed in the landing configuration.

VSR1 -The reference stalling speed in a specific configuration.

Vsw -The speed at which the onset of natural or artificial stall warning occurs.

VSTOP The highest decision speed from which the aeroplane can stop within ASDA in the event of an abandoned take-off. *AMJ 25X1591 Paragraph 3.2.1.c Note.*

VTmax The maximum safe threshold speed is the speed used to determine compliance with the landing field-length requirements. If exceeded, the required field-lengths may well exceed the landing distance available, and the approach should be immediately discontinued. The exact speed is VATo plus a pre-determined figure which is dependent on the aircraft type -usually about 15 KT. *JAR* 1 *page* 1-15.

VTmin The minimum safe threshold speed is the lowest approach speed which should be maintained at or before the threshold. It is the higher of VIMD + 5 KT or VS1g + 20%. Approaches made below this speed may result in loss of control.

Vus The speed at which the wheels of an aircraft will leave the ground if it is rotated at VR. It is often referred to as unstick speed and is the same as VLOF.

Vx The speed used to climb at the maximum gradient of climb. If the climb is to be with one-engine-inoperative for three- or four-engined aircraft then the speed is referred to as Vx1.

Vy The speed used to climb at the maximum rate of climb. If the climb is to be with one-engine-inoperative for three- or four-engined aircraft then the speed is referred to as Vy1.

Vyse The speed used to climb at the maximum rate of climb in a twin-engined aeroplane with one-engine-inoperative.

VZF The minimum safe manoeuvring speed with zero flap. This speed is used in noise abatement procedures. *ICAO DOC* 8168 *PANS-OPS Volume* 1 *page* 5-5.

CRANFIELD AVIATION TRAINING SCHOOL LTD. PART-FCL ATO N° 276
CATS INNOVATION CENTRE, LUTON, Bedfordshire LU2 8DL U.K.

www.catsaviation.com

7-6

Performance